The
Custer
Adventure

The
Custer

Adventure

As Told by its Participants

Stories Selected and Edited by

RICHARD UPTON

Illustrated by

J. K. Ralston

UPTON AND SONS

El Segundo, California   1990

LIBRARY OF CONGRESS CARD CATALOG #90-70274
ISBN: 0-912783-20-6 (hardcover)
ISBN: 0-912783-19-2 (softcover)

Upton and Sons - Publishers
917 Hillcrest St.
El Segundo, CA 90245

CONTENTS

In Memory of
JAMES SCOTT UPTON
1965-1979
We love you, Jim!

Introduction

It has been said that Napoleon is the only military leader that has been the subject of more books, paintings and miscellaneous literature than George Armstrong Custer. With the Custer Battle Centennial in 1976 and the added interest in the battle and the man that this event inspires, Custer may well become history's most written about military figure. With so much literature available about this relatively unimportant event the bewildered reader may well find himself in a labyrinth of material that presents all manner of theories, biographies of all the major, minor and peripheral characters, scholarly dissertations, efforts of journalistic scavengers and even whole volumes written about the horse who was found alive but badly wounded on the battlefield.

The purpose of this book is to present to the reader a factual, interesting and exciting account of the Custer Adventure using stories as recorded and remembered by the actual participants in this epic event.

All of the main points of the Custer Battle will be mentioned in chronological order starting with Mrs. Custer's emotion packed description of the flag-flying, band-playing column leaving Fort Abraham Lincoln on May 17, 1876 to the return to the same place by the black be-decked steamer *Far West* on the fifth of July bringing confirmation to the rumor that Custer's cavalry had met disaster as evidenced by the wounded troopers of the Seventh Cavalry on its' decks.

Using diaries, letters, official reports, newspaper interviews and previously published, but difficult to obtain, material the reader will be led step by step to the inevitable conclusion at the Battle of the Little Big Horn and its' aftermath.

It is hoped that information recorded in this book will provide a solid background to someone who has time to read only one Custer book and maybe this work will stimulate the reader to investigate more thoroughly the events and the men and women who helped shape them.

The art work in this book was created by the eminent Montana artist J. K. Ralston whose main forte is historical authenticity. The stories herein tell, as Mr. Ralston says, "the red meat," of the Custer fight, and his illustrations contribute magnificently to the telling and understanding of the story.

The stories that were selected to tell the Custer Adventure were chosen because they are the "red meat." The accounts were recorded by people who were there. One did not survive the disaster, the others' lives were forever changed because of the trauma of the death of the nation's most heralded cavalry leader and five troops of the gallant Seventh Cavalry while the United States celebrated its' Centennial year — 1876.

George Custer is still a controversial character as he was during his active career. Maybe his reputation as an Indian fighter wasn't entirely justified but his Civil War record more than established his reputation as a dynamic leader of men and for a capacity to get things accomplished.

Certainly Custer was not the psychotic fool as portrayed in the movie *Little Big Man* nor was he the super hero of *They Died With Their Boots On*, but curiously he is almost always placed in one of these two extreme categories — hero or fool.

At the time of Lt. Colonel George Custer's death he was our country's most famous military leader. He was a genuine celebrity with lucrative offers to lecture and write of his exciting experiences. He was married to a beautiful young woman who, after her husband's death, wrote three books that helped immortalize her husband and firmly establish him as a legend.

Custer wrote in his book, *My Life on the Plains*, "If I were an Indian, I often think I would greatly prefer to cast my lot among those of my people adhered to the free open plains rather than submit to the confined limits of a reservation, there to be the recipient of the blessed benefits of civilization, with its vices thrown in without stint or measure." Hardly the thoughts of a psychotic fool.

2

Here then is the story of the Custer Adventure by the woman who loved him, the men who died with him, the men who survived him and the men who buried him.

This is the way it happened at the Little Big Horn.

Chapter One

Leaving Fort Abraham Lincoln May 17, 1876

The Treaty of 1868 was signed at Fort Laramie and brought to a close Red Cloud's War. The Sioux and Cheyennes had forced the closing of the Bozeman Trail and with it the Forts Reno, Phil Kearny and C. F. Smith that guarded it. The Indians were granted by the terms of the treaty, "that country north of the North Platte River and east of the summits of the Big Horn Mountains." Located within this somewhat indefinite area were the Black Hills. The Black Hills, or Pa Sapa, the sacred hills, were the Indians' holy land and when, in the summer of 1874, Lt. Colonel George Custer led an expedition into this area the Indians were rightfully upset. Geologists with the Custer expedition discovered gold in the Black Hills, and when news of this discovery became known the stampede of prospectors to this Indian land began. For a while the army tried to enforce the terms of the treaty and keep the miners and prospectors out of the area. This failing, the government attempted to purchase the region. The Sioux put, what the government considered, a ridiculously high price on the region and would not listen to a counter offer by the government. These efforts being unsuccessful it was decided by both military and civilian leaders that war could only be avoided by returning all the Indians to their reservations. An order to this effect was issued by the Commissioner of Indian Affairs in December of 1875. Using historical perspective, today we can

5

see that this decision instead of bringing peace provoked the war of 1876.

After warning the Indians to return to their reservations and the Indians failing to heed, and in some cases even being aware of, the ultimatum, the military acted. The plan originated at the Headquarters of the Military Division of the Missouri in Chicago. Three separate military units would be put in the field with orders to "bring Sitting Bull's band and other wild and lawless Indians residing without the bounds of their reservation back to their reservation to which they were assigned and to do it by force."

Colonel John Gibbon would lead the Second Cavalry and Seventh Infantry east from Fort Ellis, Montana with about 500 men. General George Crook would march north from Fort Fetterman where he was reorganizing his command after a not so successful engagement with Cheyenne Indians on the Little Powder River in March of 1876. He had about 1,000 soldiers of the Second and Third Cavalry and Fourth and Ninth Infantry with him.

Leaving Fort Abraham Lincoln and heading west would be the Dakota column that numbered about 900 soldiers that included the entire twelve troops of the Seventh Cavalry, portions of the Sixth, Seventeenth and Twentieth Infantry. The Dakota column was *not* commanded by Lt. Colonel George A. Custer.

Custer had incurred the wrath of President Ulysses S. Grant by testifying in March of 1876 at the Heister Clymer committee investigation of corruption in the administration of traderships in the Indian country. Custer's testimony implicated the President's brother Orvil Grant and when Custer's testimony was shown to be only heresay evidence the President reacted, through a series of political moves, by relieving Custer from the command of the pending expedition that was organizing at Fort Abraham Lincoln and furthermore ruling that Custer not accompany the outfit at all.

President Grant finally relented to pressure from General Alfred H. Terry, the commander of the Department of Dakota, and Lt. General Philip H. Sheridan, commanding the Division of the Missouri, that Custer be allowed to accompany the Dakota column, but only if General Terry personally retain the command of the expedition.

So now the stage was set. The three columns, (the Montana column under the command of Colonel John Gibbon, the Dakota column led by General Alfred H. Terry, with Custer smarting under the rebuke by President Grant, and the General Crook column coming up from the South), were expected to find the Indians and force them to return to their reservations.

We begin our Custer Adventure with a moving, emotion packed account of the Seventh Cavalry's departure from Fort Abraham Lincoln on May 17, 1876, by Mrs. Elizabeth B. Custer.

For the next fifty-seven years until her death on April 6, 1933, Mrs. Custer devoted her life to the memory of her gallant husband. It has been said that by tacit agreement between survivors and students of the battle that, out of respect for Mrs. Custer, no criticism of her husband's part in the battle would be made public until her death. Part of the reason for much of the mystery surrounding the Custer fight is that Mrs. Custer outlived all but one of the leading participants in the controversy. Colonel Charles A. Varnum, a lieutenant at the time of the fight and in charge of the Indian scouts, died on February 26, 1936.

Elizabeth Custer wrote three books about her adventures as the wife of Lt. Colonel George A. Custer. They are *Tenting on the Plains, Following the Guidon* and *Boots and Saddles.* From her first book, *Boots and Saddles,* published in 1885, the following portion of our Custer Adventure is quoted.

"The morning for the start came only too soon. My husband was to take Sister Margaret[1] and me out for the first day's march, so I rode beside him out of camp. The column that followed seemed unending. The grass was not then suitable for grazing, and as the route of travel was through a barren country, immense quantities of forage had to be transported. The wagons themselves seemed to stretch out interminably. There were pack mules, the ponies already laden, and cavalry, artillery, and infantry followed, the cavalry being in advance of all. The number of men, citizens, employees, Indian scouts, and soldiers was about twelve hundred. There were nearly seventeen hundred animals in all.

"As we rode at the head of the column, we were the first to enter the confines of the garrison. About the Indian quarters, which we were obliged to pass, stood the squaws, the old men, and the children singing, or rather moaning, a minor tune that has been uttered on the going out of Indian warriors since time immemorial. Some of the squaws crouched on the ground, too burdened with their trouble to hold up their heads; other restrained the restless children, who, discerning their fathers, sought to follow them.

"The Indian scouts themselves beat their drums and kept up their peculiar monotonous tune, which is weird and melancholy beyond description. Their war-song is misnamed when called music. It is more of a lament or a dirge than an inspiration to activity. This intoning they kept up for miles along the road. After we had passed the Indian quarters we came near Laundress Row,[2] and there my heart entirely failed me. The wives and children of the soldiers lined the road. Mothers, with streaming eyes, held their little ones out at arm's length for one last look at the departing father. The toddlers among the children, unnoticed by their elders, had made a mimic column of their own. With their handkerchiefs tied to sticks in lieu of flags, and beating old tin pans for drums, they strode lustily back and forth in imitation of the advancing soldiers. They were fortunately too young to realize why the mothers wailed out their farewells.

"Unfettered by conventional restrictions, and indifferent to the opinion of others, the grief of these women was audible, and was accompanied by desponding gestures, dictated by their bursting hearts and expressions of their abandoned grief.

"It was a relief to escape from them and enter the garrison, and yet, when our band struck up 'The Girl I Left Behind Me,' the most despairing hour seemed to have come. All the

8

sad-faced wives of the officers who had forced themselves to their doors to try and wave a courageous farewell, and smile bravely to keep the ones they loved from knowing the anguish of their breaking hearts, gave up the struggle at the sound of the music. The first notes made them disappear to fight out alone their trouble, and seek to place their hands in that of their Heavenly Father, who, at such supreme hours, was their neverfailing solace.

"From the hour of breaking camp, before the sun was up, a mist had enveloped everything. Soon the bright sun began to penetrate this veil and dispel the haze, and a scene of wonder and beauty appeared. The cavalry and infantry in the order named, the scouts, pack-mules, and artillery, and behind all the long line of white-covered wagons, made a column altogether some two miles in length. As the sun broke through the mist a mirage appeared, which took up about half of the line of cavalry, and thenceforth for a little distance it marched, equally plain to the sight on the earth and in the sky.

"The future of the heroic band, whose days were even then numbered, seemed to be revealed, and already there seemed a premonition in the supernatural translation as their forms were reflected from the opaque mist of the early dawn.

"The sun, mounting higher and higher as we advanced, took every little bit of burnished steel on the arms and equipments along the line of horsemen, and turned them into glittering flashes of radiating light. The yellow, indicative of cavalry, outlined the accouterments, the trappings of the saddle, and sometimes a narrow thread of that effective tint followed the outlines even up to the headstall of the bridle. At every bend of the road, as the column wound its way round and round the low hills, my husband glanced back to admire his men, and could not refrain from constantly calling my attention to their grand appearance.

"The soldiers, inured to many years of hardship, were the perfection of physical manhood. Their brawny limbs and lithe, well-poised bodies gave proof of the training their outdoor life had given. Their resolute faces, brave and

9

confident, inspired one with a feeling that they were going out aware of the momentous hours awaiting them, but inwardly assured of their capability to meet them.

"The general could scarcely restrain his recurring joy at being again with his regiment, from which he had feared he might be separated by being detained on other duty. His buoyant spirits at the prospect of the activity and field-life that he so loved made him like a boy. He had made every plan to have me join him later on, when they should have reached the Yellowstone.

"The steamers with supplies would be obliged to leave our post and follow the Missouri up to the mouth of the Yellowstone, and from thence on to the point on that river where the regiment was to make its first halt to renew the rations and forage. He was sanguine that but a few weeks would elapse before we would be reunited, and used this argument to animate me with courage to meet our separation.

"As usual we rode a little in advance and selected the camp, and watched the approach of the regiment with real pride. They were so accustomed to the march the line hardly diverged from the trail. There was a unity of movement about them that made the column at a distance seem like a broad dark ribbon stretched smoothly over the plains.

"We made our camp the first night on a small river[3] a few miles beyond the post. There the paymaster made his disbursements, in order that the debts of the soldiers might be liquidated with the sutler.

"In the morning the farewell was said, and the paymaster took sister and me back to the post.

"With my husband's departure my last happy days in garrison were ended, as a premonition of disaster that I had never known before weighed me down. I could not shake off the baleful influence of depressing thoughts. This presentiment and suspense, such as I had never known, made me selfish, and I shut into my heart the most uncontrollable anxiety, and could lighten no one else's burden. The occupations of other summers could not even give temporary interest."

10

Chapter Two

The March to Rosebud Creek
May 17, 1876 — June 21, 1876

The May 17th entry in the diary of Dr. James M. DeWolf reads, in part ". . . marched 12 miles on the Little Heart River . . . Mrs. Custer came this far."

On October 23, 1875, Dr. James M. DeWolf signed a one year contract with the army to serve in the Department of Dakota. As Acting Assistant Surgeon, U.S. Army, he was assigned to the 7th Cavalry and reported to Lt. Colonel George A. Custer at Fort Abraham Lincoln on March 2, 1876.

While he served with the Dakota column he kept an informative diary that is particularly interesting and useful to historians of this period. DeWolf, in addition to his diary wrote often to his considerably younger wife, Fannie, and recounted in more detail his feelings for her and his expectations of the military expedition. In several of his letters he states that "the column is unlikely to see an Indian this summer."

Dr. DeWolf's diary along with his letters was donated to the Custer Battlefield National Monument by Dr. Verne A. Dodd, son of Mrs. DeWolf by her second marriage.

Brig. General Alfred H. Terry, at the suggestion of Gen. Sheridan was in command of the Dakota column. Terry entered the Union Army from the state of Connecticut where he had been a licensed attorney.

He capped a brilliant Civil War career by leading his forces in the capture of Fort Fisher, a major confederate stronghold in January of 1865.

Capitalizing on his training in law and his administrative skills Terry remained in the army after the war and rose to become the commander of the Department of Dakota.

General Terry never before had any Indian fighting experience and that could be the reason he interceded on Custer's behalf when it appeared that George Custer might not be allowed to accompany the expedition.

Terry's field diary kept during this period reveals a certain frustration with some of his subordinates, notably Lt. Colonel Custer and Major Marcus A. Reno, both of whom acted independently without orders even before any Indians were seen or the planned rendezvous with the Montana Column under Colonel John Gibbon was accomplished.

Custer had a habit of assuming leadership roles and, as Terry wrote, "playing wagonmaster," and once left the column in an attempt to find a better trail "without any authority whatever."

Reno's improvisations of his orders during his scout up Powder River and vicinity will be commented on later in our story.

General Terry, while unquestionably brilliant in other areas and a gentleman of the first order, seemed unable to earn the respect of Lt. Colonel Custer and when it really counted could not demand it.

The writings of Dr. DeWolf and General Terry tell this portion of the Custer Adventure. From the official report of General Alfred H. Terry found in the House of Representatives Executive Document 1, Part 2, 44th Congress, 2nd Session, Report of the Secretary of War . . . Volume 1, Washington, D.C. 1876 we quote the following. ". . . For some days its [the column's] progress was slow, for the wagons were heavily laden and recent rains had made the ground extremely soft.

"The Little Missouri was reached on May 29. Here a halt was made for a day in order that the valley of the river might be reconnoitered. This was done by Lt. Colonel Custer with a portion of his regiment, but no indications of the recent presence of Indians were discovered. The march was resumed on the 31st; but on the 1st and 2nd of June a heavy snow-storm detained the column on the edge of the bad lands which border the left banks of the Little Missouri. On the 3rd Beaver Creek was reached. In the morning of that day scouts, sent out by Major [Orlando] Moore from the Yellowstone, brought me dispatches from that officer and from Colonel Gibbon [the Montana Column] also. From the scouts I learned that there were no traces of Indians between "Stanley's Stockade"[1] and Beaver Creek; by the dispatches I was informed that the steamers[2] with supplies had reached their destination, and that Colonel Gibbon, having received the dispatch sent to him from Fort Lincoln, was marching down the Yellowstone. Upon this information I determined to move up Beaver Creek, and thence march directly to Powder River. Orders were therefore sent to Colonel Gibbon to suspend his movements and to Major Moore to send one boat-load of supplies to the mouth of the Powder.

"On the morning of the 4th the march was again resumed, our course being up the Beaver. On the 6th we turned again to the west, and in the evening of the 7th reached Powder River at a point about twenty miles from the Yellowstone.

"On the 8th, leaving the column in camp, I went with an escort to the mouth of the Powder, and there found the steamer *Far West* with supplies.

"The next day I went on the steamer up the Yellowstone to meet Colonel Gibbon. I met him at a point ten or fifteen miles below the mouth of the Tongue, and gave him instructions to return with his troops to the mouth of the Rosebud. Returning, I gave orders for the transfer of all troops and supplies from Stanley's Stockade to a depot to be established at the mouth of the Powder, and thence proceeded to the camp of the column.

"The next day, June 10, Major M. A. Reno, Seventh Cavalry, with six companies of his regiment and one Gatling gun, was directed to reconnoiter the valley of the Powder as far as the forks of the river, then to cross to Mizpah Creek, to descend that creek to near its mouth, thence to cross to Tongue River and *descend to its mouth* [italics this editor's].

13

He was provided with rations for ten days, carried on pack-saddles. On the 11th the remainder of the column marched to the Yellowstone, where it remained until the 15th, in order to give time for Major Reno's movements. During this interval the troops at the stockade, and all the supplies which had been landed there, were brought up.

"On the morning of the 15th, Lt. Colonel Custer, with six companies of his regiment, one Gatling gun, and a train of pack-mules, marched for Tongue River, all the wagons with their infantry-guard having been left at the depot. He reached the Tongue on the 16th. Here we waited for news from Major Reno until the evening of the 10th,[3] when a dispatch was received from him, by which it appeared that he had crossed to the Rosebud and found a heavy Indian trail; and that after following it for some distance he had retraced his steps, had descended the stream [the Rosebud] to its mouth, and was then on his way to the Tongue.[4] Orders were at once sent to him to halt and await the arrival of Lt. Colonel Custer; and the latter was instructed to march the next morning for the mouth of the Rosebud. He arrived at this last-named point on

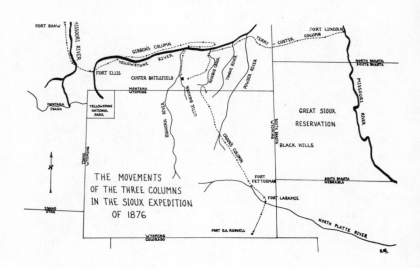

THE MOVEMENTS
OF THE THREE COLUMNS
IN THE SIOUX EXPEDITION
OF 1876

the 21st. On the same day Colonel Gibbon's column was put in motion for a point on the north bank of the Yellowstone, opposite the mouth of the Big Horn; with it were sent the Gatling guns which had until this time accompanied the Seventh Cavalry. [5]

"At a conference which took place on the 21st between Colonel Gibbon, Lt. Colonel Custer, and myself, I communicated to them the plan of operations which I had decided to adopt. It was that Colonel Gibbon's column should cross the Yellowstone near the mouth of the Little Big Horn, [6] and thence up that stream, with the expectation that it would arrive at the last-named point by the 26th; that Lt. Colonel Custer with the whole of the Seventh Cavalry should proceed up the Rosebud until he should ascertain the direction in which the trail discovered by Major Reno led; that if it led to the Little Big Horn it should not be followed; but that Lt. Colonel Custer should keep still farther to the south before turning toward that river, in order to intercept the Indians should they attempt to pass around his left, and in order, by a longer march, to give time for Colonel Gibbon's column to come up.

"This plan was founded on the belief that at some point on the Little Big Horn a body of hostile Sioux would be found; and that although it was impossible to make movements in perfect concert, as might have been done had there been a known fixed objective point to be reached, yet, by the judicious use of the excellent guides and scouts which we possessed, the two columns might be brought within co-operating distance of each other, so that either of them which should be first engaged might have a "waiting fight" — give time for the other to come up. At the same time it was thought that a double attack would very much diminish the chances of a successful retreat by the Sioux, should they be disinclined to fight. It was believed to be impracticable to join Colonel Gibbon's column to Lt. Colonel Custer's force; for more than one-half of Colonel Gibbon's troops were infantry, who would be unable to keep up with cavalry in a rapid movement; while to detach Gibbon's mounted men and add

15

them to the Seventh Cavalry would leave his force too small to act as an independent body."

On June 21, 1876 Dr. James M. DeWolf, a civilian contract surgeon took time out to write what turned out to be his last letter to his wife. The next morning all twelve companies of the Seventh Cavalry moved out in search of the Indian trail.

Dr. DeWolf's letter has been puncuated and capitalized where necessary in order that the reader will not be distracted by grammatical errors. The substance and content remain the same however.

Yellowstone, Mouth of Rosebud Creek
June 21st 76

"Darling wife

. . . [We] are fitting up for a scout under [Brevet] General Custer with 12 companies of cavalry up the Rosebud, across to the Big Horn River & down that to the Yellowstone . . . We marched about 25 miles a day, in all about 285 miles.[7] I and Dr. [Henry R.] Porter[8] messed together and had a nice time. We had just been getting a supply for the next scout. The commissary is a very good supply on the boat. We found no Indians, not one. All old trails. They seem to be moving west and are driving the buffalo. I think it is very clear that we shall not see an Indian this summer. The post-trader or John Smith has opened his whiskey &, of course, you all know what will follow for the time we remain here.[9] [Brevet] General Gibbon's command is encamped opposite us.[10] The boat will take our battery over to him this evening.[11] It has hurt three men already (the battery) by upsetting. Dr. [George E.] Lord[12] has joined us and will take Dr. [John Winfield] Williams' place as Chief Medical Officer on this scout . . .

"We usually start at 5 A.M. and march until 1 or 2 P.M. which is not hard and is fun when there is any trail but I fear we shall not find even a sign that is new this time. It is believed that the Indians have scattered and gone back to their reservations. Yesterday I went out with Dr. Porter, Lt. [Henry M.] Harrington[13] and Lt. [Benjamin H.] Hodgson[14] pistol shooting and came out second best, Porter was best, so you see some of the cavalry cannot shoot very well. Hodgson & I are harassing (joking etc.) each other & have some nice times. He is Adjutant of the Right Wing "6" Companies of Cavalry. Reno's command. I hope when we return from this scout we shall be nearly ready to return, then darling only think, we will have 300 or 400 miles to march home again. We had two cases of *slight* sunstrokes (it was before the whiskey was opened) . . . Rosebud Creek takes its name by being profusely bordered by the wild roses like those of Warner. I send you one in this letter . . . Well darling, I must close this as the boat moves down the river some little distance & the mail closes tonight & I want to be sure this goes in this mail for it has been 11 days since I wrote or had a chance to write. You must remember darling that one feels pretty tired after getting into camp and then we have so much to do to fit up again for this. Everything goes on pack mules & dirt is plentiful. Love & kisses darling. My regards to all. from your loving Hub

J M DeWolf"

Dr. DeWolf was killed by Indians on June 25, 1876, during the retreat of Major Reno and his command across the Little Big Horn River. He became separated from the other soldiers when he attempted to ride up a ravine a little to the north of the others, was cut off, killed and scalped in full view of some of his comrades whose testimonies are recorded in the transcript of the 1879 Reno Court of Inquiry.

His friend Dr. H. E. Porter, the only doctor to survive the battle, wrote Mrs. DeWolf a letter on July 28, 1876, in which he sensitively wrote the following. ". . . I was just behind him as we crossed the river. I saw him safe across and then he turned up a ravine a little to my left which was the last I saw of my friend and companion — alive. As soon as we reached the bluff, I found he was missing and soon found his body which I had buried the next day. I know it will be a great

17

relief to you when I say that his body was not mutilated in the least — that he was not scalped or his clothes even taken. The Indians had stolen his revolver but not troubled him otherwise . . ."

Chapter Three

Rosebud Creek to Reno's Crossing
June 22, 1876 - June 25, 1876

First Lieutenant Edward Settle Godfrey commanded Company K, Seventh Cavalry and fought vigorously during the defense of Reno Hill on June 25-26, 1876.

Godfrey, as the years went by following the battle, became determined to write, what he felt would be, an authoritative word on the fight.

He returned ten years later to the battlefield in 1886 and stayed at nearby Fort Custer. Fort Custer was built in 1877, a year after the battle. While at the ten year anniversary reunion of survivors of the battle he had a marvelous opportunity to interview participants of the battle, both red and white alike.

As a result of Lt. Godfrey's research he wrote an article entitled, "Custer's Last Battle," which was published in the January 1892 issue of *The Century Magazine*. Godfrey's interest in the battle never faltered and he returned to the battlefield in 1906, 1916 and again in 1926. He was a favorite in later years with Mrs. Custer and was a leader in the first Indian War Veteran's Organizations.

Shortly before the Seventh Cavalry marched up the Rosebud, General Alfred H. Terry wrote out his instructions to Lt. Colonel George Custer. Since that time students of the Custer fight have debated whether these instructions represented orders or suggestions to the leader of the Seventh Cavalry. Strong arguments have been made by both sides of

19

the controversy but no clear cut verdict has been generally agreed upon.

Following these written instructions to Custer from Terry we will quote portions of Lt. Godfrey's January 1892 *Century Magazine* article as he, Godfrey, describes the march up the Rosebud. Lt. Godfrey refers to Lt. Colonel Custer by his brevet or honorary rank of general throughout the article. Godfrey constantly refers to the units as "Troops" which in 1892 was quite accurate. During Custer's time the units were called "Companies." In 1882 Cavalry units were changed from Company to Troop.

"General Custer's written instructions were as follows:

Camp at Mouth of Rosebud River
Montana Territory, June 22nd, 1876

Lieut. Col. Custer, 7th Cavalry
Colonel:

The Brigadier-General Commanding directs that, as soon as your regiment can be made ready for the march, you will proceed up the Rosebud in pursuit of the Indians whose trail was discovered by Major Reno a few days since. It is, of course, impossible to give you any definite instructions in regard to this movement, and were it not impossible to do so, the Department Commander places too much confidence in your zeal, energy, and ability to wish to impose upon you precise orders which might hamper your action when nearly in contact with the enemy. He will, however, indicate to you his own views of what your action should be, and he desires that you should conform to them unless you shall see sufficient reason for departing from them. He thinks that you should proceed up the Rosebud until you ascertain definitely the direction in which the trail above spoken of leads. Should it be found (as it appears almost certain that it will be found) to turn towards the Little Horn, he thinks that you should still proceed southward, perhaps as far as the headwaters of the Tongue, and then turn towards the Little Horn, feeling constantly, however, to your left, so as to preclude the possibility of

20

the escape of the Indians to the south or southeast by passing around your left flank. The column of Colonel Gibbon is now in motion for the mouth of the Big Horn. As soon as it reaches that point it will cross the Yellowstone and move up at least as far as the forks of the Big and Little Horns. Of course its future movements must be controlled by circumstances as they arise, but it is hoped that the Indians, if upon the Little Horn, may be so nearly inclosed by the two columns that their escape will be impossible.

The Department Commander desires that on your way up the Rosebud you should thoroughly examine the upper part of Tullock's Creek, and that you should endeavor to send a scout through to Colonel Gibbon's column, with information of the result of your examination. The lower part of the creek will be examined by a detachment from Colonel Gibbon's command. The supply steamer will be pushed up the Big Horn as far as the forks if the river is found to be navigable for that distance, and the Department Commander, who will accompany the column of Colonel Gibbon, desires you to report to him there not later than the expiration of the time for which your troops are rationed, unless in the meantime you receive further orders.

> Very respectfully,
> Your obedient servant,
> E. W. Smith, Captain, 18th Infantry,
> Acting Assistant Adjutant-General

"At twelve o'clock, noon, on the 22nd of June, the 'Forward' was sounded, and the regiment marched out of camp in column of fours, each troop followed by its pack mules. Generals Terry, Gibbon and Custer stationed themselves near our line of march and reviewed the regiment. General Terry had a pleasant word for each officer as he returned the salute. Our pack-trains proved troublesome at the start, as the cargoes began falling off before we got out of camp, and during all that day the mules straggled badly. After that day,

21

however, they were placed under the charge of Lieutenant [Edward G.] Mathey, who was directed to report at the end of each day's march the order of merit of the efficiency of the troop packers. Doubtless, General Custer had some ulterior design in this. It is quite probable that if he had had occasion to detach troops requiring rapid marching, he would have selected those troops whose packers had the best records. At all events the efficiency was much increased, and after we struck the Indian trail the pack trains kept well closed. We went into camp about 4 P.M., having marched twelve miles. About sunset 'officer's call' was sounded, and we assembled at General Custer's bivouac and squatted in groups about the General's bed. It was not a cheerful assemblage; everybody seemed to be in a serious mood, and the little conversation carried on, before all had arrived, was in undertones. When all had assembled, the General said that until further orders, trumpet calls would not be sounded except in an emergency; the marches would begin at 5 A.M. sharp; the troop commanders were all experienced officers, and knew well enough what to do, and when to do what was necessary for their troops; there were two things that would be regulated from his headquarters, i.e. when to move out of and when to go into camp. All other details, such as reveille, stables, watering, halting, grazing, etc., on the march would be left to the judgment and discretion of the troop commanders; they were to keep within supporting distance of each other, not to get ahead of the scouts, or very far to the rear of the column. He took particular pain to impress upon the officers his reliance upon their judgment, discretion, and loyalty. He thought, judging from the number of lodge-fires reported by Reno, that we might meet at least a thousand warriors; there might be enough young men from the agencies, visiting their hostile friends, to make a total of fifteen hundred. He had consulted the reports of the Commissioner of Indian Affairs and the officials while in Washington as to the probable number of 'Hostiles' (those who had persistently refused to live or enroll themselves at the Indian agencies), and he was confident that there would not be an opposing force of more

22

than fifteen hundred. General Terry had offered him the additional force of the battalion of the 2nd Cavalry, but he had declined it because he felt sure that the 7th Cavalry could whip any force that would be able to combine against him, that if the regiment could not, no other regiment in the service could; if they could whip the regiment, they would be able to defeat a much larger force, or, in other words, the reinforcement of this battalion could not save us from defeat. With the regiment acting alone, there would be harmony, but another organization would be sure to cause jealousy or friction. He had declined the offer of the Gatling guns for the reason that they might hamper our movements or march at a critical moment, because of the inferior horses and of the difficult nature of the country through which we would march. The marches would be from twenty-five to thirty miles a day. Troop officers were cautioned to husband their rations and the strength of their mules and horses, as we might be out for a great deal longer time than that for which we were rationed, as he intended to follow the trail until we could get the Indians, even if it took us to the Indian agencies on the Missouri River or in Nebraska. All officers were requested to make to him any suggestions they thought fit.

"This 'talk' of his, as we called it, was considered at the time as something extraordinary for General Custer, for it was not his habit to unbosom himself to his officers. In it he showed concessions and a reliance on others; there was an indefinable something that was *not* Custer. His manner and tone, usually brusque and aggressive, or somewhat curt, was on this occasion conciliating and subdued. There was something akin to an appeal, as if depressed, that made a deep impression on all present. We compared watches to get the official time, and separated to attend to our various duties. Lieutenants [Donald] McIntosh, [George D.] Wallace[1] and myself walked to our bivouac, for some distance in silence, when Wallace remarked: 'Godfrey, I believe General Custer is going to be killed.' 'Why, Wallace?' I replied, 'What makes you think so?' 'Because,' said he, 'I have never heard Custer talk in that way before.'

"I went to my troop and gave orders what time the 'silent' reveille should be and as to other details for the morning preparations; also the following directions in case of a night attack; the stable guard, packers, and cooks were to go out at once to the horses and mules to quiet and guard them; the other men were to go at once to a designated rendezvous and await orders; no man should fire a shot until he received orders from an officer to do so. When they retired for the night they should put their arms and equipments where they could get them without leaving their beds. I went through the herd to satisfy myself as to the security of the animals. During the performance of this duty I came to the bivouac of the Indian scouts. 'Mitch' Bouyer, the half-breed interpreter, 'Bloody Knife,' the chief of the Arikara Ree scouts;[2] 'Half-Yellow-Face' the chief of the Crow scouts, and others were having a 'talk.' I observed them for a few minutes, when Bouyer turned toward me, apparently at the suggestion of 'Half-Yellow-Face' and said, 'Have you ever fought against these Sioux?' 'Yes,' I replied. Then he asked, 'Well, how many do you expect to find?' I answered, 'It is said we may find between one thousand and fifteen hundred.' 'Well, do you think we can whip that many?' 'Oh, yes, I guess so.' After he had interpreted our conversation, he said to me with a good deal of emphasis, 'Well, I can tell you we are going to have a damned big fight.' At five o'clock sharp, on the morning of the 23rd, General Custer mounted and started up the Rosebud, followed by two sergeants, one carrying the regimental standard, and the other his personal or head-quarters flag, the same kind of flag he used while command-ing his cavalry division during the Civil War. This was the signal for the command to mount and take up the march. Eight miles out we came to the first of the Indian camping-places. It certainly indicated a large village and numerous population. There were a great many 'wickiups' (bushes stuck in the ground with the tops drawn together, over which they placed canvas or blankets). These we supposed at the time were for the dogs, but subsequent events developed the fact that they were temporary shelters of the transients from the agencies. During the day we passed through three of these camping-places and made halts at each one. Everybody was busy studying the age of the pony droppings and tracks and lodge trails, and endeavoring to determine the number of lodges. These points were all-absorbing topics of conversation. We went into camp about five o'clock, having marched about thirty-three miles.

"June 24th we passed a great many camping places, all appearing to be of nearly the same strength. One would naturally suppose these were the successive camping places of the same village, when, in fact, they were the continuous camps of the several bands. The fact that they appeared to be of nearly the same age, that is, having been made at the same time, did not impress us then. We passed through one much larger than any of the others. The grass for a considerable distance around it had been cropped close, indicating that large herds had been grazed there. The frame of a large 'Sun-Dance' lodge was standing, and in it we found the scalp of a white man. It was whilst here that the Indians from the agencies had joined the Hostiles' camp. The command halted here and the 'officers' call' was sounded. Upon assembling we were informed that our Crow scouts, who had been very active and efficient, had discovered fresh signs, the tracks of three or four ponies and one Indian on foot. At this point a stiff southerly breeze was blowing; as we were about to separate, the General's headquarters' flag was blown down, falling toward our rear. Being near the flag I picked it up and stuck the staff in the ground, but it again fell to the rear. I then bored the staff into the ground where it would have the support of a sagebrush. This circumstance made no impression on me at the time, but after the battle, an officer, Lieutenant Wallace, asked me if I remembered the incident. He had observed, and regarded the fact of its falling to the rear as a bad omen, and felt sure we would suffer a defeat.

"The march during the day was tedious. We made many long halts, so as not to get ahead of the scouts, who seemed to be doing their work thoroughly, giving special attention to the right, toward Tulloch's Creek, the valley of which was in

25

general view from the divide. Once or twice signal smokes were reported in that direction, but investigation did not confirm the reports. The weather was dry and had been for some time, consequently the trail was very dusty. The troops were required to march on separate trails, so that the dust clouds would not rise so high. The valley was heavily marked with lodge-pole trails and pony tracks, showing that immense herds of ponies had been driven over it. About sundown we went into camp under the cover of a bluff, so as to hide the command as much as possible. We had marched about twenty-eight miles. The fires were ordered to be put out as soon as supper was over, and we were to be in readiness to march again at 11:30 P.M.

"Lieutenant [Luther R.] Hare and myself lay down about 9:30 to take a nap. When comfortably fixed, we heard someone say, 'He's over there by that tree.' As that described my location pretty well, I called out to know what was wanted, and the reply came: 'The General's compliments, and he wants to see all the officers at headquarters immediately.' So we gave up our much-needed rest and groped our way through horse herds, over sleeping men, and through thickets of bushes trying to find headquarters. No one could tell us, and as all fires and lights were out we could not keep our bearings. We finally espied a solitary candle-light, toward which we traveled and found most of the officers assembled at the General's bivouac. The General said that the trail led over the divide to the Little Big Horn; the march would be taken up at once, as he was anxious to get as near the divide as possible before daylight, where the command would be concealed during the day, and give ample time for the country to be studied, to locate the village, and to make plans for the attack on the 26th. We then returned to our troops, except Lieutenant Hare, who was put on duty with the scouts. Because of the dust, it was impossible to see any distance and the rattle of equipments and clattering of the horses' feet made it difficult to hear distinctly beyond our immediate surroundings. We could not see the trail and we could only follow it by keeping in the dust cloud. The night was very calm, but occasionally a slight breeze would waft the cloud and disconcert our bearings; then we were obliged to halt to catch a sound from those in advance, sometimes whistling or hallooing, and getting a response we could start forward again. Finally, troopers were put ahead, away from the noise of our column, and where they could hear the noise of those in front. A little after 2 A.M., June 25th, the command was halted to await further tidings from the scouts; we had marched about ten miles. Part of the command unsaddled to rest the horses. After daylight some coffee was made, but it was impossible to drink it; the water was so alkaline that the horses refused to drink.

"Some time before eight o'clock, General Custer rode bareback to the several troops and gave orders to be ready to march at eight o'clock, and gave information that scouts had discovered the locality of the Indian village or camps in the valley of the Little Big Horn, about twelve or fifteen miles beyond the divide. It was from this divide between the Little Big Horn and Rosebud that the scouts had discovered the smoke rising above the village, and the pony herds grazing in the valley of the Little Big Horn, somewhere about twelve or fifteen miles away.[3] It was to their point of view that General Custer had gone while the column was halted in the ravine.[4] It was impossible for him to discover more of the enemy than had already been reported by the scouts. In consequence of the high bluffs which screened the village, it was not possible in following the trail to discover more. Nor was there a point of observation near the trail from which further discoveries could be made until the battle was at hand.

"Just before setting out on the march, I went to where General Custer's bivouac was. The General, 'Bloody Knife,' and several Ree scouts and a half-breed interpreter were squatted in a circle, having a 'talk' after the Indian fashion. The General wore a serious expression and was apparently abstracted. The scouts were doing the talking, and seemed nervous and disturbed. Finally 'Bloody Knife' made a remark that recalled the General from his reverie, and he asked in his usual quick, brusque manner, 'What's that he says?' The

27

interpreter replied: 'He says we'll find enough Sioux to keep us fighting two or three days.' The General smiled and remarked, 'I guess we'll get through with them in one day.'

"We started promptly at eight o'clock and marched uninterruptedly until 10:30 a.m. when we halted in a ravine and were ordered to preserve quiet, keep concealed, and not do anything that would be likely to reveal our presence to the enemy. We had marched about ten miles . . .

"It was well known to the Indians that the troops were in the field, and a battle was fully expected by them; but the close proximity of our column was not known to them until the morning of the day of the battle. Several young men had left the hostile camp on that morning to go to one of the agencies in Nebraska. They saw the dust made by the column of troops; some of their number returned to the village and gave warnings that the troops were coming, so the attack was not a surprise.[5] For two or three days their camp had been pitched on the site where they were attacked. The place was not selected with the view to making that the battle-field of the campaign, but, whoever was in the van on their march thought it a good place to camp, put up his tepee, and the others as they arrived followed his example. (This was [Sioux Chief] Gall's explanation.) It is customary among the Indians to camp by bands. The bands usually camp some distance apart, and Indians of the number then together would occupy a territory of several miles along the river valley, and not necessarily within supporting distance of each other. But in view of the possible fulfillment of Sitting Bull's prophecy[6] the village had massed . . .

"Our officers had generally collected in groups and discussed the situation. Some sought solitude and sleep, or meditation. The Ree scouts, who had not been very active for the past day or two, were together and their 'medicine man' was anointing them and invoking the Great Spirit to protect them from the Sioux. They seemed to have become satisfied that we were going to find more Sioux than we could well take care of. Captain [George W.] Yates' troop[7] had lost one of its packs of hard bread during the night march from our

28

last halting place on the 24th. He had sent a detail back on the trail to recover it. Captain [Myles W.] Keogh came to where a group of officers were and said this detail had returned and Sergeant [William] Curtis, in charge, reported that when near the pack they discovered an Indian opening one of the boxes of hard bread with his tomahawk, and that as soon as the Indian saw the soldiers he galloped away to the hills, out of range and then moved along leisurely. This information was taken to the General at once by his brother, Captain Tom Custer. The general came back and had 'officers' call' sounded. He recounted Captain Keogh's report, and also said that the scouts had seen several Indians moving along the ridge overlooking the valley through which we had marched, as if observing our movements; he thought the Indians must have seen the dust made by the command. At all events, our presence had been discovered and further concealment was unnecessary; that we would move at once to attack the village; that he had not intended to make the attack until the next morning, the 26th, but our discovery made it imperative to act at once, as delay would allow the village to scatter and escape. Troop commanders were ordered to make a detail of one non-commissioned officer and six men to accompany the pack; to inspect their troops and report as soon as they were ready to march; that the troops would take their places in the column of march in the order in which reports of readiness were received; the last one to report would escort the pack-train.

"The inspections were quickly made and the column was soon en route. We crossed the dividing ridge between the Rosebud and Little Big Horn valleys a little before noon. Shortly afterward the regiment was divided into battalions. The advance battalion, under Major Reno, consisted of Troop 'M', Captain [Thomas H.] French; Troop 'A', Captain [Myles] Moylan and Lieutenant Varnum and Hare, and the interpreter [Frederick F.] Girard; Lieutenant Hodgson was Acting Adjutant, and Doctors DeWolf and Porter were the medical officers. The battlion under General Custer was composed of Troop 'I', Captain Keogh and Lieutenant [James E.] Porter; Troop 'F', Captain Yates and Lieutenant

[William V. W.] Reily; Troop 'C', Captain [Thomas W.] Custer and Lieutenant Harrington; Troop 'E', Lieutenants [Algernon E.] Smith and [James G.] Sturgis; Troop 'L', Lieutenants [James] Calhoun and [John H.] Crittenden; Lieutenant [William W.] Cooke was the Adjutant, and Doctor G. E. Lord was medical officer. (It was thought by some that Custer's troops were divided into two battalions, one under Captain Keogh and one under Captain Yates.) The battalion under Captain [Frederick W.] Benteen consisted of Troop 'H', Captain Benteen and Lieutenant [Francis M.] Gibson; Troop 'D', Captain [Thomas B.] Weir and Lieutenant [Winfield S.] Edgerly, and Troop 'K', Lieutenant Godfrey. The pack-train, Lieutenant Mathey in charge, was under escort of Troop 'B', Captain [Thomas M.] McDougall.

"Major Reno's battalion marched down a valley that developed into the south branch of the small tributary to the Little Big Horn, now called 'Sun-Dance,' Benteen's or Reno Creek. The Indian trail followed the meanderings of this valley. Custer's column followed Reno's closely, bearing to the right and rear. The pack-train followed their trail.

"Benteen's battalion was ordered to the left and front, to a line of high bluffs about three or four miles distant. Benteen was ordered if he saw anything, to send word to Custer, but to pitch into anything he came across; if, when he arrived at the high bluffs, he could not see any enemy, he should continue his march to the next line of bluffs and so on until he could see the Little Big Horn Valley.

"There is no doubt that Custer was possessed with the idea that the Indians would not 'stand' for a daylight attack, that some of them would try to escape up the valley of the Little Big Horn with families, ponies and other impedimenta, and if so, he wanted them intercepted and driven back toward the village. This idea and another that the village might be strung out along the valley for several miles were probably the ones that influenced him to send Benteen's battalion to the left. Benteen marched over a succession of rough steep hills and deep valleys. The view from the point where the regiment was organized into battalions did not discover the difficult nature

30

of the country, but as we advanced farther, it became more and more difficult. To save the strain on the battalion, Lieutenant Gibson was sent some distance in advance, but saw no enemy, and so signaled the result of his reconnaissance to Benteen. The obstacles threw the battalion by degrees to the right until we came in sight of and not more than a mile from the trail. Many of our horses were greatly jaded by the climbing and descending, some getting far into

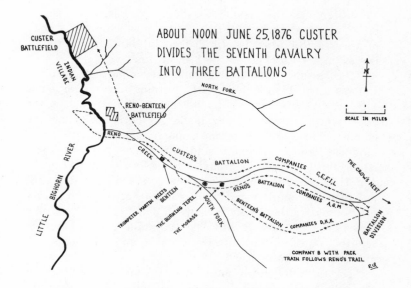

ABOUT NOON JUNE 25,1876 CUSTER DIVIDES THE SEVENTH CAVALRY INTO THREE BATTALIONS

the rear of the column. Benteen very wisely determined to follow the trail of the rest of the command, we got into it just in advance of the pack-train. During this march on the left, we could see occasionally the battalion under Custer, distinguished by the troop mounted on gray horses, marching at a rapid gait. Two or three times we heard loud cheering and also some few shots, but the occasion of these demonstrations is not known. Some time after getting on the trail we came to a waterhole, or morass, at which a stream of running

31

water had its source, Benteen halted the battalion. While watering, we heard some firing in advance, and Weir became impatient at the delay of watering and started off with his troop, taking the advance, whereas his place in column was second. The rest of the battalion moved out very soon afterward and soon caught up with him. We were now several miles from the Reno battlefield or the Little Big Horn. Just as we were leaving the water-hole, the pack-train was arriving, and the poor thirsty mules plunged into the morass in spite of the efforts of the packers to prevent them, for they had not had water since the previous evening.[8] We passed a burning tepee, fired presumably by our scouts, in which was the body of a warrior who had been killed in the battle with Crook's troops on the Rosebud on the 17th of June.

"The battalions under Reno and Custer did not meet any Indians until Reno arrived at the burning tepee; here a few were seen. These Indians did not act as if surprised by the appearance of troops; they made no effort to delay the column, but simply kept far enough in advance to invite pursuit. Reno's command and the scouts followed them closely until he received orders to 'move forward at as rapid a gait as he thought prudent, and charge the village afterward, and the whole outfit would support him.' According to Reno's official report this order was given him near this burning tepee. He says: 'Lieutenant Cooke, adjutant, came to me and said the village was only two miles above, and running away,' and gave the above order.

"The Little Big Horn bottom, down which the trail led, is generally flat, and from one to two miles wide; along the stream, especially in the bends at the time of the fight, it was heavily timbered, principally large cotton woods, and obstructed a view of the main villages until Reno got to where he made his farthest advance down the valley; here the village loomed up large among the cottonwoods below. Reno, following the Indian trail, crossed at a ford; about three and a half miles below it, in a direct line, is a second ford; between these fords, skirting the right bank and paralleling the river is a ridge from one hundred to three hundred feet above the valley, which rises abruptly from river and valley. In following the summit of this ridge the travel distance is considerably increased. The northeast slope declines rather gently at the upper end, but more abruptly at the lower end, and drains into a usually dry stream bed which joins the river at the second ford. About two miles below this ford is another. These lower fords were used by the hostiles in swarming to the attack on Custer's troops.

"Reno's battalion moved at a trot to the river, where he delayed about ten or fifteen minutes watering the horses and reforming the column on the left bank of the stream; both Captain Keogh and Lieutenant Cooke were at this crossing for a short time.[9] Reno now sent word to Custer that he had everything in front of him, and that the enemy was strong."

Chapter Four

Reno's Fight In The Valley

As the opening stages of the battle were about to begin, the Seventh Cavalry found itself divided into four separate units. Major Reno had just crossed the Little Big Horn River and was about to charge down the valley towards the Indian village with his three companies, (A, G and M), and the Arikara Indian scouts, about 140 men in all.

About this time Captain Benteen, finding no Indian signs on what he called his "valley hunting" scout to the left, had returned to follow Custer's freshly made trail that was leading to the valley of the Little Big Horn. He had Trumpeter Martin's message from Custer ordering him, Benteen, to "come quick" securely in his shirt pocket. Benteen had Companies H, D and K, about 125 men, under his command. He did not know that Custer had sent Reno to charge the village.

The water-starved pack train under the command of Captain Thomas M. McDougall, Company B, was struggling in the morass about a mile to the rear of Benteen.

Lt. Colonel George Custer retained command of the remaining five companies, (C, E, F, I and L), of the Seventh. After ordering Reno across the river and into the valley, Custer and his 220 men turned to the right and disappeared from the view of Reno's troops following a course downstream, the exact route of which will never be known.

At this point the spotlight shifted to Major Marcus A. Reno who would spend the rest of his life explaining, defending and rationalizing the decisions that he would make in the valley of the Little Big Horn. While Reno had earned a reputation during the Civil War as a brave officer whose war record included many commendations for "gallant and meritorious services," this day would give him his first experience in Indian fighting. Edgar Stewart, a respected historian, has described Reno as one who, "demonstrated that the courage to follow is one thing, while the courage to lead is something very different."

Because of the extent of the negative criticism that Major Reno received in the years following the Custer fight the Major requested that a hearing be held so "that the many rumors started by camp gossip may be set at rest and the truth made fully known." A Court of Inquiry convened at Chicago, Illinois on January 13, 1879 and adjourned February 11, 1879 during which the testimonies of twenty-three witnesses were heard and many documentary exhibits were received in evidence. The finding of the court failed to satisfy completely either the pro-Custer or anti-Custer factions when it ruled that, "The conduct of the officers throughout was excellent and while subordinates in some instances did more for the safety of the command by brilliant displays of courage than did Major Reno, there was nothing in his conduct which requires animadversion from this court."

After crossing the river Reno's battalion entered a narrow band of trees and halted there to re-form. It was at this point that Reno became aware that the Sioux were not running but were coming up to meet him. Major Reno dispatched unlucky Trooper Archibald McIlhargey with a message to Lt. Colonel Custer to tell him of this fact. McIlhargey was killed with Custer.

Second Lieutenant Charles A. Varnum, Company A, was in command of the detachment of Indian scouts whose purpose was to trail the enemy and capture or run off the pony herds of the Sioux. As the fourth witness called at the Reno Court of Inquiry in 1879, Varnum described the action during Reno's fight in the valley as follows.

". . . The village was situated along the left bank of the Little Big Horn. Owing to the bend in the stream and the timber around on the left bank of the stream, it was almost

35

impossible unless you got well out on the plain to see much of the village in coming from the direction that we came . . . I don't think I ever made any figures on the strength of the Indians until the fight was pretty well over, but there were certainly more Indians than I ever saw together before . . . I had seen immense numbers of Indians from the tops of the bluffs I was on when I was out scouting, and I knew there was a very large village there, indeed . . . There were 8 or 10 Indian scouts with me at the time, and as soon as the column passed I was joined by Lieutenant Hare, who had been detailed to assist me in scouting. We started out 50 to 75 yards ahead of the command. The [valley] bottom opened out wider as we went down the stream. There was quite a large body of Indians some little distance off . . . running back and forth across the prairie . . . apparently trying to kick up all the dust they could, and it was so covered with dust it was impossible to discover the number of Indians there . . . I noticed all of a sudden that they stopped and turned backward, and I turned my head around and glanced back to see the cause, and I noticed a battalion deploying from column into line, and I supposed at the time that they [the Indians] supposed they [the soldiers] were going to halt, and turned back on us at that time. The command then moved forward again in line and we rode on, I suppose, 50 yards in front, . . . and as we went down the [valley] we worked out toward the bluffs, toward the left of Major Reno's line. The Indians let us come closer and closer as we came down . . . and as we worked toward the left we could see quite a number of tepees . . . We went on down possibly two miles, and the line halted and dismounted[1] . . . When the line halted, I rode with Lieutenant Hare, [back] toward the line, and the Indian scouts, as they generally fight in Indian fashion were gone and I don't know where[2] . . . My old company was in the line (Capt. Moylan's Company A) and I went back and reported to him and told him I should stop with his company during the fight. The [skirmish] line was then deployed perpendicularly to the general direction of the river, and the skirmish immediately commenced between the Indians and the troops.

36

In looking up to the bluffs on our immediate right — right across the general direction of the river, I saw the Gray Horse Company of the battalion moving along the bluffs, and as I know now the Gray Horse Company was with Custer, I suppose it was his command. General Custer always rode a very fast-walking horse that would make the whole command trot when he was riding at the head of the column; and I just think that was the gait at which the command was moving. I do not say that General Custer was necessarily riding that particular horse, but that is my impression about the gait . . .

"When I had been on the line 10 or 15 minutes I heard somebody say that 'G' Company was going to charge a portion of the village down through the woods, or something to that effect . . . I was on my horse and rode down into the

"I saw the Gray Horse Company . . . moving along the bluffs . . ."
Courtesy, Big Horn County Bank, Hardin, Montana

timber to go with the company that was going to charge the village. In the timber there is a little glade or opening, and I know in riding into this opening I could see the stream in one direction . . . and could see that there was a detached portion of the village on the other side of the stream, and that is where they were going. I heard no order. It was just a rumor that I followed, and I saw Major Reno there.[3] He was right with 'G' Company, evidently deploying it, or assisting to deploy it to go through the woods . . . The line at that time appeared to have fallen back to the edge of the timber, that is, it was lying on the edge of the timber instead of being perpendicular to it. The command was riding in the timber, and I could not see all of the men. I saw Captain Moylan first when I got onto the edge of the line, and he called out . . . that the horses we had dismounted from were beyond the left flank of our line, the Indians were circling into the timber toward his left flank and would cut off our horses, and all our extra ammunition was there, and something must be done . . . I dismounted then, and as I did so I heard Captain Moylan call out that his men were out of ammunition, and he ordered each alternate man should fall back from the line and get ammunition out of their saddle-bags, and return so as to let the others go back and get ammunition from their saddle-bags. Then I got up to the right of the line and met Mr. Girard and Charley Reynolds, and stopped and talked with them I guess about a minute or two or three minutes, when I heard from the woods cries of 'Charge!! Charge!! We are going to charge!' There was quite a confusion, — something about a charge down in the woods, and I jumped up and said: 'What's that?' and started down into the woods and grabbed my horse. Everybody was mounted. I didn't hear any orders . . . I have no idea how the order to charge or fall back was communicated to the troops.[4] I heard some men yelling that they were going to charge, or something like that. In reference to the danger to the command I would say that it was hardly a safe place. They were fighting a force of Indians who outnumbered them, and there was that danger . . . Whether the bullets came from the bluffs above or from the

38

bottom I don't know, but I know that quite a lively shower came in from our rear toward the river. I don't know that any efforts were made to ascertain where that firing from the rear came from. I don't know that any point was designated where the command should rally or retreat on. The point to which Major Reno retreated, taking the road we went, was about 400 yards from the crossing. It is right up a steep hill on a straight line. It was about three-quarters of a mile from the crossing to the place in the woods where the skirmish line was formed. It took the troops about 6 or 7 minutes to reach the crossing on the retreat. When we came out of the woods I came out on the left of the column, and there were a great many Indians scampering along with their rifles across the saddle, working their Winchesters on the column. When we got to the top of the hill most of the Indians withdrew. Between us and the stream I saw 15 or 20 in the timber, and I have understood since that there were several bodies found there where I saw the Indians dodging and running through

". . . there were a great many Indians scampering along with rifles across the saddle, working their Winchesters on the column."

that light brush.[5] On the retreat some of the troops were using their revolvers. On the retreat the command had to go into the river on the jump, because it is a straight bank down to the water, and on coming out on the other side I know my horse nearly threw me off, he jumped up so straight. I don't know whether any of the men fell back into the river there. When I got out of the river I turned to the left, and some of the men called to me to come back. They could see Indians up there that I couldn't see. Dr. DeWolf was going in that direction, and I called to him to come back. He had just started to do so when he was shot. I do not know that the crossing was covered during the retreat. There were not many shots fired there, but I think several men were killed there; among them was Corporal Dallas [James Dalious]. That firing must have come from the hill above us. I saw the shot fired from there that killed Dr. DeWolf, and I saw him fall.

"A cavalry charge may be made in columns of two or fours, — or in line. If it was a charge with the force at Major Reno's disposal to pass through a body of Indians, I think a column of fours would be a very good formation; it would give the men an opportunity to use their revolvers. With the number of Indians in our front, I think I would rather have it a little closer than a column of fours . . . as green as some of ours were. After riding 100 yards in a column of fours, the men would not all be in their places; some horses travel faster than others, anyhow. The column went across the bottom at a fast gallop, but not so fast as they could have gone. I had to slow my horse down with the bit to keep him along with the head of the column. I had a very good horse. When we came out of the woods every man was going on his own hook, and that was why I spoke to them about running, but when I saw the officer in command I understood the matter.[6] At the first crossing the water was about four and a half to five feet deep. The Indians did not follow us clear to the river, I think, for the firing receded as we came down to the river. On the retreat almost everybody I saw was considerably excited — and they were considerably excited when they went in, for that matter. They were very much demoralized when they got

40

on the hill after the retreat, — but they had left a good many behind them, and the command was not handled there as it was when they were taken in."

The Death of Isaiah Dorman
"We passed a black man in a soldier's uniform and we had him."
Courtesy, John M. Carroll

Chapter Five

Left In The Valley

When Major Marcus A. Reno gave the orders to halt the charge to the Indian village and for the troopers to dismount and fight on foot, any plan that Lt. Colonel George A. Custer may have had for the units to attack in concert and achieve victory was doomed to failure. Custer promised to support Reno "with the whole outfit" and it is reasonably certain that he, Custer, was riding downstream to attack the village at some other point. To further seal the fate of George Custer and his five troops of the Seventh Cavalry, Reno's retreat, or charge as the Major insisted on calling it, from the valley floor to a defensive position atop the bluffs on the other side of the Little Big Horn River freed practically all of the Indians to meet the threat of the Custer column that appeared downstream on the flank of the village.

Left in the valley, along with Custer's hope of victory, were four men who, in the confusion of the retreat, were cut off from the river crossing and forced to take cover in the thin band of timber and brush beside the river. They were Frederick F. Girard, the civilian interpreter for the Indian scouts, William (Billy) Jackson, a half-blood Blackfoot, Private Thomas O'Neill of Company G and First Lieutenant Charles Camilus DeRudio. Each of these survivors recorded their adventures in various publications and one, William Jackson, was the subject of a full length book by James Willard Schultz entitled *William Jackson, Indian Scout*.

Lieutenant Charles DeRudio described his ordeal in a letter dated July 5, 1876 written from a camp on the north side of the Yellowstone. Using this letter, which was published in the

42

New York Herald on July 30, 1876 and portions of DeRudio's 1879 Reno Court of Inquiry testimony we present this unusual story. First, from the New York Herald letter:

"I had a narrow escape at the battle of the Little Big Horn on the 25 and 26 of June and I will endeavor to give you my experience of Indian fighting."

DeRudio then describes Reno's fight in the valley and proceeds to tell the circumstances that led to his being left behind during Reno's retreat.

". . . The fire from the numerically superior force necessitated a retreat which was almost impossible, as we were now surrounded by warriors. When we entered the engagement we were only 100[1] strong and the fire of the enemy had made havoc in our little band. When we were half way over the creek, I, being in the rear, noticed a guidon planted on the side we had left and returned to take it. When coming through the wood, the guidon entangled itself in the branches and slipped out of my hand. I dismounted to pick it up and led my horse to the south bank of the creek. As I was about to mount, my horse was struck with a bullet, and becoming frightened, he ran into the Indians, leaving me dismounted in the company of about 300 Sioux not more than 50 yards distant. They poured a whistling volley at me, but I was not wounded, and managed to escape to the thicket nearby, where I would have an opportunity of defending myself and selling my life at a good high figure. In the thicket I found Mr. Girard, the interpreter; a half-breed Indian [William Jackson]; and Private O'Neill, of Company G, 7th Cavalry. The first two of the quartet had their horses, while O'Neill, like myself, was dismounted. I told the owners of the horses that the presence of the animals would betray us, suggesting at the time that they be stampeded. They declined to act on the suggestion and I left them and crawled through the thick underwood into the deep dry bottom of the creek, where I could not easily be discovered, and from whence I hoped to be able under cover of darkness to steal out and rejoin the command."

At the Reno Court of Inquiry in 1879 Lieutenant DeRudio

43

testified that "About two minutes after Major Reno's command got on top of the hill, I heard an immense volley firing on the other side of the river, north of the village, down the river.[2] It was about 4 or 5 miles from the place where I was. As I was up the stream in the valley I was more apt to hear it. That firing lasted probably an hour and a half, and then died off in small shots, and pretty soon the fire passed away entirely. Some of the Indians who had left Major Reno came right back, and part went over the bluffs and part went to the right across the plain down to the south side of Major Reno." [End of Reno Court testimony, letter to the New York Herald cont.]

". . . I heard a crackling noise near me, which upon investigation I found proceeded from burning wood, the Indians having ignited a fire. The wood being very dry, the fire made rapid headway, and I was forced from my hiding place. I crawled out of the creek bottom the same way I had approached, and as I was about to ascend the bank, I heard a voice calling, 'Lieutenant, Lieutenant.' I could see no one, but the call was repeated, and advancing a few yards in the direction from which it proceeded, I found all three of the party I had left a short time before, hidden in the bottom of the creek. Mr. Girard told me he had left the horses tied together, where I had seen them, and followed down after me. I found that the party, like myself, was afraid of the progress of the fire; but fortunately for us, the wind subsided, and a little rain fell which, thank God, was sufficient to arrest the flames and revive our hope that we might be able to remain there until night. It was now 3 o'clock P.M.: six more hours to wait, and you may imagine how immensely long we found them. During this time we could hear and often see Indians around us and could hear them talk quite near us . . . Finally the time came when under the protection of night (it was very cloudy) we were able to come out of our hiding places and take the direction of the ford, which was two miles to the south, through an open plain. Mr. Girard and the scout [Jackson] mounted their horses and the soldier and myself took hold, each one, of a horse's tail, and

44

followed them. Mr. Girard proposed that, in case he should be obliged to run and leave us, and succeeded in joining the command, he would notify Major Reno, the commander, of my position. During our transit through the open plain we passed many Indians returning to their village and could hear but not see them as the night was very dark. We reached the wood near what we took to be the ford we had passed in the morning, but we were mistaken and had to hunt for the crossing. Once we forded the stream but found it was at a bend and that we would have to ford it again. When we recrossed the river, we ran full into a band of eight savages. The two mounted men ran for their lives, the soldier and myself jumped into the bushes near us. I cocked my revolver and in a kneeling position was ready to fire at the savages if they should approach me. They evidently thought, from the precipitate retreat of the two mounted men, that all of us had decamped; and began to talk among themselves . . . We then saw that all the fords were well guarded by the savages, and it would be very dangerous to attempt to cross any part of the river . . . The night passed and in the dim dawn of day we heard an immense tramping, as of a large cavalry command, and the splashing of the water convinced us that some troops were crossing the river. I imagined it was our command, as I could distinctly hear the sound of the horses' shoes striking the stones. I cautiously stepped to the edge of the bushes to look out (I was then no more than three yards from the bank of the river), and thought I recognized some gray horses mounted by men in military blouses, and some of them in white hats. They were, I thought, going out of the valley, and those that had already crossed the river were going up a very steep bluff, while others were crossing after them. I saw one man with a buckskin jacket, pants, top boots and white hat, and felt quite sure I recognized him as Captain [Tom] Custer which convinced me that the cavalry-men were of our command.

"With this conviction I stepped boldly out on the bank and called to Captain Custer, 'Tom, don't leave us here.' The distance was only a few yards and my call was answered by an infernal yell and a discharge of 300 or 400 shots.[3] I then discovered my mistake and found the savages were clad in clothes and mounted on horses which they had captured from our men. Myself and the soldier jumped into the bushes (the bullets mowing down the branches at every volley), and crawled off to get out of range of the fire. In doing so we moved the top branches of the undergrowth, and the Indians on the top of the bluff fired where they saw the commotion and thus covered us with their rifles. We now decided to cross a clearing of about twenty yards and gain another wood; but before doing this, I took the precaution to look out. The prospect was terribly discouraging for on our immediate right, not more than fifty yards distant, I saw four or five Indians galloping toward us. Near by me there were two cottonwood stumps nearly touching each other, and behind this slender barricade myself and the soldier knelt down, he with his carbine and I with my revolver, ready to do for a few of the savages before they could kill us . . . They had not seen us and when the foremost man was just abreast of me and about ten yards distant, I fired. They came in Indian file, and at my fire they turned a right-about and were making off when Private O'Neill fired his carbine on the second savage, who at that moment was reining his pony to turn him back. The private's eye was true, and his carbine trusty, for Mr. Indian dropped his rein, threw up his paws and laid down on the grass to sleep his long sleep. The gentleman I greeted rode a short distance and then did likewise. The rest of the party rode on, turned the corner of the wood and disappeared . . . During all this time the fire from the bluffs continued, but after we had fired our shots, it ceased, and we retired to the thicket . . . From our position we could see the Indians on the bluffs, their horses picketed under the cover of the hill, and a line of sharpshooters, all lying flat on their stomachs. We could hear the battle going on above us on the hills,[4] the continued rattle of the musketry, the cheering of our command, and the shouting of the savages. Our hopes revived when we heard the familiar cheer of our comrades, but despondency followed fast for we discovered that our

46

wood was on fire . . . and we had to shift our position. We crawled almost to the edge of the wood, when we discovered that the fiends had fired both sides. We moved around until we found a thick cluster of what they call bulberry trees, under which we crept. The grass on the edge of this place was very green, as it has been raining a little while before, and there was no wind. When the fire approached our hiding place it ran very slowly so that I was enabled to smother it with my gauntlet gloves. The fire consumed all the underwood around us and was almost expended by this time.

"There we were in a little oasis, surrounded by fire, but comparatively safe from the elements, and with the advantage of seeing almost everything around us without being seen. We could see savages going backward and forward, and one standing on picket not more than 70 or 80 yards from us, evidently put there to watch the progress of the fire. At about 4 o'clock P.M. this picket fired 4 pistol shots in the air at regular intervals from each other and which I interpreted as a signal of some kind. Soon after this fire we heard the powerful voice of a savage crying out, making the same sound four times, and after these two signals, we saw 200 or more savages leave the bluffs and ford the river, evidently leaving the ground. About one hour after, the same double signals were again repeated, and many mounted Indians left at a gallop. Soon the remainder of those left on the bluffs also retired.

"Hope now revived, the musketry rattle ceased and only now and then we could hear a far off shot. By 6 o'clock everything around us was apparently quiet and no evidence or signs of any Indians were near us. We supposed the regiment had left the field, and all that remained for us to do was to wait for the night and then pass the river and take the route for the Yellowstone River, and there construct a raft and descend to the mouth of the Powder River, our supply camp. Of course during the 36 hours that we were in suspense, we had neither water nor food. At 8 P.M. we dropped ourselves into the river, the water reaching our waists, crossed it twice and then carefully crawled up the bluffs, took our direction and slowly and cautiously proceeded southward.

"After marching two miles, I thought I would go up on a very high hill to look around and see if I could discover any sign of our command; and on looking around I saw a fire on my left and in the direction where we supposed the command was fighting during the day, probably two miles from us. Of course we made two conjectures on this fire; it might be an Indian fire and it might be from our command. The only way to ascertain was to approach it cautiously and trust to chance. Accordingly we descended the hill, and took the direction of the fire. Climbing another and another hill, we listened a while and then proceeded on for a mile or more, when on the top of a hill we again stopped and listened. We could hear voices, but not distinctly enough to tell whether they were savages or our command. We proceeded a little farther and heard the bray of a mule, and soon after, the distinct voice of a sentry challenging with the familiar words, 'Halt; Who goes there?' The challenge was not directed to us, as we were too far off to be seen by the picket, and it was too dark; but this gave us courage to continue our course and approach, though carefully, lest we should run into some Indians again. We were about 200 yards from the fire and . . . I cried out, 'Picket, don't fire; it is Lieutenant DeRudio and Private O'Neill,' and started to run. We received an answer in a loud cheer from all the members of the picket and Lieutenant Varnum. This officer, one of our bravest and most efficient, came at once to me and was very happy to see me again, after having counted me among the dead; . . ."

Chapter Six

On Reno Hill

As the beaten remnants of Reno's battalion reached the top of the bluffs Captain Frederick Benteen and his three companies came upon the scene. Benteen still did not know that Custer had divided the column again and had sent Reno across the river with orders to charge the village. Trumpeter John Martin, Custer's last known messenger, while searching for Benteen had, from the high bluffs, briefly viewed Reno's fight in the valley. Incomprehensibly Martin failed to mention this to Benteen. Even when Benteen pointed out to Martin that the trumpeter's horse was wounded, Martin still did not mention that the last he saw of the Custer command was when they were galloping down into the ravine with the gray horse troop in the center and that Indians were waving buffalo robes and firing from ambush at Custer.

Martin, a 25 year old Italian immigrant with language difficulties, had given the impression, when he told Benteen the Indians had "skedaddled" that the attack was successful and the soldiers had captured the Indian village.

As Benteen drew closer to the river he could see hundreds of Indian warriors chasing the stragglers of Reno's command and immediately realized that whatever had happened the soldiers had become the hunted instead of the hunters.

Rather than cross the river and head down the valley, Benteen, as Custer had done earlier, turned to his right toward the bluffs. Reno, spying Benteen's column approaching, rode to meet it and pleaded, "For God's sake, Benteen, halt your command and help me. I've lost half my men." Reno, at this point had 32 killed, 10-11 wounded and 19 missing.

Benteen, even though he had Custer's order to "Come quick" in his pocket, halted his unit and joined up with Reno. It is possible and even probable that by this decision Benteen saved the remaining seven companies of the Seventh Cavalry from annihilation. It is also possible that Benteen could have saved Custer's command by making a vigorous attack on the Indians at the right psychological moment and turned the tide of battle.

At any rate Benteen's decision to support Reno's battalion was the final blow to any chance Custer had of survival let alone victory. By the time an attempt was made to locate Custer it was too late as the Indians were finished with the Custer command and were about to turn their full attention to the soldiers on Reno Hill.

Benteen, a Civil War standout and Seventh Cavalry member since 1866, had a gift of leadership that inspired the men who served under him. These qualities of leadership and bravery were demonstrated again and again by Benteen as he inspired by both example and deed the demoralized troopers of Reno's command.

John Ryan was First Sergeant of Company M and was in both the valley and Reno hill fights. Ryan enlisted in the Union Army in 1861 and served in the Seventh Cavalry from 1866 to 1876. In 1923 he wrote an account of his experiences during Reno's fight at the Little Big Horn. His story was written exclusively for the Billings (Mont.) Gazette and the Hardin (Mont.) Tribune. We quote portions of his story that appeared on June 25, 1923 in the Gazette.

". . . After we gained the bluffs we could look back upon the plains where the Indians were, and could see them stripping and scalping our men, and mutilating their bodies in a horrible manner. The prairie was all afire. The officers did all in their power to rally the men, and while they were doing so many were killed.

"After the companies were formed the firing ceased,[1] and we were joined by Benteen's battalion, which was the first we had seen of him since the division of the regiment. Soon

50

after, the pack train arrived, with Company B, under Captain McDougall, which was very fortunate, as our ammunition was nearly exhausted, and we could not get supplies from any other source. We had several wounded men and we attended to them as well as circumstances would permit. I understood at that time that Captain Weir with his Company D, left the command there, and started in the direction General Custer took for a short distance, and then returned, although I did not see him.[2]

"Leaving two companies with the packs and wounded, Major Reno, with five companies, or what was left of them, proceeded in the direction we had supposed General Custer took, and in the direction of the Indian camp.

"We went in that direction for probably half a mile until we gained a high point[3] and could overlook the Indian camp and the battlefield. We saw at a distance of from a mile and a half to two miles parties whom we supposed were Indians, riding back and forth, firing scattering shots. We thought that they were disposing of Custer's wounded men, and this afterward proved to be true.[4]

"We halted for a few moments, and saw a large herd of ponies at the further end of the village, and could distinguish a large party of Indians coming towards the Indian camp. The prairie around the village and the first battlefield was all afire, having been set by the Indians to hide their movements.

"At the top of this bluff we halted, and at the foot there was a ford, and this was where Custer had first encountered the Indians, as we found some of the dead bodies there two days afterwards.[5] While we were on the bluffs the Indians again made their appearance, coming in large numbers from the direction in which we heard the firing. We exchanged several shots with them, and we lost a few men, and then had orders to fall back to our packs and wounded.[6]

"On our arriving there we dismounted in haste, putting the wounded in a low depression on the bluffs and put packs from the mules around them to shelter them from the fire of the Indians. We then formed a circle of our pack mules and horses, forming a skirmish line all around the hole, and then

51

"They made several charges upon us . . ."

lay down and waited for the Indians.

"We had been in this position but a short time when they advanced in great numbers from the direction in which we came.

"They made several charges upon us and we repulsed them every time. Finally they surrounded us. Soon the firing became general all along the line, very rapid and at close range. The company on the right of my company had a number of men killed in a few minutes. There was a high ridge on the right and an opening on the right of our lines, and one Indian in particular I must give credit for being a good shot.

"While we were lying in this line he fired a shot and killed the fourth man on my right. Soon afterward he fired again and shot the third man. His third shot wounded the man on my right, who jumped back from the line, and down among the rest of the wounded. I thought my turn was coming next. I jumped up, with Captain French, and some half a dozen members of my company; instead of firing straight to the front, as we had been doing up to the time of this incident, we wheeled to our right and put in a deadly volley, and I think we put an end to that Indian, as there were no more men killed at that particular spot . . .

"When dark set in, it closed the engagement on the twenty-fifth. We went to work with what tools we had, consisting of two spades, our knives and tin cups, and, in fact, we used pieces of hard tack boxes for stakes, and commenced throwing up temporary works. We also formed breastworks from boxes of hard bread, sacks of bacon, sacks of corn and oats, blankets, and in fact everything that we could get hold of.

"During the night ammunition and the rations reached us where we were entrenched in the lines, but we suffered severely from lack of water, as the Indians held the approach to it. During the night several men made attempts to get water, but they were killed or driven back.[7]

"About the middle of the night, we heard a trumpet call, and the men commenced to cheer, thinking it was Custer's

53

men who were coming to our assistance. Major Reno ordered one of our trumpeters to sound a call, but it was not repeated, so we made up our minds that it was a decoy on the part of the Indians to get us out of our works.

"The trumpet that they used probably belonged to one of Custer's trumpeters, but we did not know it at that time. We had no thought of leaving our works, as we had a number of our men wounded there, and some of them pretty badly.

"At intervals during the night we could hear the Indians riding back and forth across the river. I have an idea that they thought we were going to make a rush and get out of there.

"The next morning, being the 26th, two shots were fired just before daylight by the Indians, in rapid succession. All this time we were wondering what had become of Custer and his troops. This began the engagement of another day. In a few moments the battle raged in earnest, the Indians advancing in large numbers and trying to cut through.[8]

"Captain Benteen's company particularly was hard pressed, and the men did their utmost to repulse those Indians who were gaining ground on the troops. Captain Benteen called out to Major Reno for re-enforcements, saying: 'The Indians are doing their best to cut through my lines, and it will be impossible for me to hold my position much longer.' Captain French's Company M was immediately withdrawn from that part of the line which they occupied, and rushed to the assistance of Captain Benteen's company. Both companies made a charge on the Indians and drove them down the hill, but in doing so we lost a number of men. This section of the battlefield was a little higher than the balance of the ground.

"Had the Indians been successful, the day would have been lost, and Reno's command would have shared the fate of Custer's brave men, as Captain Benteen said afterward . . .

"Late in the day the fire of the Indians slackened, except on the point of a high bluff in the direction in which it was supposed that Custer had gone. Here the Indians put in a few well-directed shots that laid several of our men low. I do not

54

know what kind of a gun one of those Indians used, but it made a tremendous noise, and, in fact those Indians were out of range of our carbine, which were Springfields, caliber .45.

"Captain French of my company asked me if I could do anything with those Indians, as they were out of range of the carbines. I told the captain that I would try, and as I was the owner of a 15-pound Sharp's telescope rifle, caliber .45, which I had had made in Bismarck before the expedition started out, and which cost me $100. I fired a couple of shots until I got range of that group of Indians. Then I put in half a dozen shots in rapid succession, and those Indians scampered away from that point of the bluff, and that ended the firing on the part of the Indians in that memorable engagement, and the boys set up quite a cheer.

"A young warrior, coupstick in hand, dashed toward the soldier's line . . . for his efforts he was shot dead."

"... I fired into them while they remained in range ...
and those were the last shots fired in the battle of the
Little Big Horn."
From **Rhymes of a Cowboy** by J. K. Ralston

"The Indians all scampered from the bluffs across the river and moved back to their encampment. We could see them pulling down their lodges and getting ready for a hasty removal. In a short time they stripped the hides off of their lodges and left the poles standing and moved out from their camp up the valley of the Little Big Horn, and over the field where Major Reno's battalion fought in the beginning of the engagement, and where his dead lay. It was the largest body of Indians that I ever saw move together at one time.

"I have seen the Cheyennes, the Arapahoes, the Kiowas, the Apaches and the Comanches move together in the Indian territory, and in Kansas years before, while campaigning there under General Custer. I should say that there were double the number moving out from this camp.

"When they moved, the captain of my company, Thomas H. French, and I fired into them while they remained in range of our two guns, and those were the last shots fired in the battle of the Little Big Horn. That was well known by every man in Reno's battalion.

"Major Reno, Captain French, Captain Benteen, Captain McDougall, Captain Weir, Lieutenant Godfrey and, in fact all of the officers did all that they could in order to defeat the Indians, and some of the officers must have had a charmed life the way they stood up under this heavy fire.

"I think the Indians took some of our men prisoners, and when other reinforcements joined us we found what appeared to be human bones, and parts of blue uniforms, where the men had been tied to stakes and trees.[9] Some of the bodies of our officers were not found, at least not at that time. Among them were Lieutenants Harrington, Porter and Sturgis. I understood that some parts of their clothing, uniform or gauntlet gloves were found on the field, which showed that they were killed. In burying the dead many of the bodies were not identified.

"After the Indians moved out of sight we jumped out of our works, built better rifle pits, and unsaddled our horses, which had not been unsaddled since the evening of the twenty-fourth.

57

"We also took the packs from the mules. Then we got water from the river in camp kettles, and made a better shelter for the horses and wounded, for we expected that the Indians would attack us again.

"Reno's command lost, between the engagement in the bottom and the entrenchments of the bluffs, somewhere about 45 men killed and 60 wounded, which will show how desperate the engagement was. In my company, out of 45 men and horses that went into the engagement, 14 men and the second lieutenant were killed, 10 wounded, and we lost about 15 horses killed or disabled.

"That night everything was quiet as far as the Indians were concerned. The next morning at daylight we could look from the bluffs over the timber to where the Indian camp was, and we saw that it was deserted, with the exception of the lodge poles, which remained standing. On the other side, a long way off from the Indian camp, we noticed a large cloud of dust arising, and a body of either Indians or troops coming towards the Indian camp, but at the time we could not distinguish which they were."

". . . a long way off from the Indian camp we noticed a large cloud of dust arising and a body of . . . troops coming . . ."

Chapter Seven

In The Indian Village

Lt. Colonel George A. Custer had estimated that when the village was finally found he would be opposed by not more than 1500 warriors. Custer figured that the Seventh Cavalry could handle that many and they probably could. What Custer did not know was that hundreds of young warriors were leaving their reservations to join Sitting Bull. Indian agents failed to report this exodus from the reservations because they made a profit that was based directly on the number of Indians that were under their control. The more Indians recorded present the bigger the financial gain for the agent. Consequently the agent's reports reflected no unusual desertions from the reservation when, in fact, the opposite was true.

Custer's Indian scouts knew that the trail they were following was that of an immense village that held far more warriors than the Seventh Cavalry could handle.

Custer, relying on the military intelligence received at Fort Abraham Lincoln, failed to realize that the abandoned Indian campsites he was encountering represented, not a succession of daily camps, but one enormous camp that had accommodated thousands more than he had estimated. At some points the Indian trail was three hundred yards wide and well worn. The Indian scouts had pointed out that the camps seemed to be of the same age as indicated by the condition of the pony droppings, and it is not to Custer's credit that he failed to heed the scouts' warning.

By the time Custer finally saw the village it contained the combined camp of the Blackfeet, Cheyenne and the seven tribes of the Sioux nation — Teton, Yanktonnais, Uncpapa,

59

Ogallala, Sans Arc, Brule and Minneconjou. It has been estimated by some that Custer attacked a village inhabited by as many as fifteen to twenty thousand Indians of which five thousand were warriors.

A week earlier on June 17, 1876 General George Crook had met about half as many warriors from this same village in the Battle of the Rosebud. Crook had more than twice as many fighting men as Custer and Crook failed to achieve a victory. Custer did not know of Crook's fight or the size of the village when he ordered Reno, with his 140 men, to attack the village.

Indian hunting parties knew the soldiers were in the area but either did not report this news or, after the fight with Crook's troops, weren't overly concerned about them.

Although most Indian stories profess they were surprised when Reno attacked the village others say the dust cloud that Custer mistook for a fleeing enemy was actually caused by the gathering up of the immense pony herd in anticipation of battle.

Mrs. Spotted Horn Bull, an Uncpapa woman, was present in the Indian village when Reno attacked. She was a highly intelligent Indian woman, who, even 25 years later, never changed her original story. Her account of the battle appeared in the St. Paul (Minn.) Pioneer Press on May 19, 1883, and we include portions of her recollections of the Custer fight that appeared in that story. With her husband at her side she told this story to a correspondent of the Pioneer Press.

". . . Eleven days before the Custer fight the Sioux were encamped some distance from the Little Big Horn . . . and a solemn sun dance was held, traces of which were afterwards seen by the troops. Though long ago absolved from partaking of its pains and penalties, Sitting Bull, the medicine man and counsellor more than the warrior, was one of those tied to the pole of suffering, and the pierced muscles of his breast still show the scars of that dire observance. One by one the others broke their bonds or succumbed to pain and fasting, but he — not trying especially to tear away — seemed rapt in study.

60

Two days and two nights went by without a morsel of food or a drop of water passing his lips, and on the morning of the third day he fainted. During his trance his faithful squaws and friends . . . forced food and drink between his lips, and when he revived, and strength returned, he told, most solemnly, of a dream in which it had been foreshadowed to him that his people were soon to meet Custer and his followers, and would annihilate them. Two mornings after this revelation, and seven before the Custer fight, just as dawn was breaking, a large force of Crows attacked the Sioux, and all day long the battle lasted[1] . . . The next morning the Sioux encampment was broken and moved to the fertile valley of the Little Big Horn . . .

"The bodies [Indian Rosebud Battle fatalities] had been brought to the new encampment . . . and were placed in a tepee[2] on the extreme right, or south, of the town of tepees, which soon spread for nearly five miles along the river, and on its western bank . . .

"Asked as to the number of warriors the seven tribes mentioned mustered at the time, Mrs. Spotted Horn Bull was unable to give a definite estimate, but her husband . . . said 5,000 would cover the braves and chiefs. This number is probably correct or nearly so, as it agrees with computations of the best posted scouts who saw the encampment before and after the fight . . . The [Little Big Horn] river runs nearly north at the scene of the fight. The ground on the west bank, where the Indians were camped, is level, and the five tribes on the north were on the flat near the river, the other two being on the first bench — a rise of from four to six feet — while above them to the west and south the plain extends. On the east side of the river, where the troops approached, the hills are precipitous and . . . where Reno threw up his shallow earthworks, . . . an altitude of at least 200 feet is attained . . . The descent into the river from the side on which were the Indians, is over a bank only a few feet in sheer height, but on the bluff side the shore rises at an angle of more than 45 degrees. Only thoroughly panic-stricken troops could have scaled such an acclivity, and the reason all were not killed is explained by . . . [Mrs. Spotted Horn Bull] later, when she tells of the counter panic among the reds. The ride up the hills to the breast works is steep, but not markedly so, and the retreating troops made it in good time for tired horses . . . Riverward, . . . is a moderately dense chapparel of willows and cottonwoods. On the plain above, trees are few. Where Custer fell, . . . the ground is high and treeless but rolling, and the descent to the river is not as steep as farther south . . .

"The Indian woman continued her account . . . 'Very early in the morning of the day of the fight (June 25) seven Cheyennes started southwest to join Spotted Tail. Five of them, it would seem, got through all right, but early in the morning two rode to the brow of the bluffs and signaled with their blankets that white troops in large numbers were advancing rapidly. The troops seen by the scouts were Custer's, for immediately after the signalling, and while the camp was in commotion, Reno's command came up, unseen by most of the Indians, from the south and on the western side of the river, and opened fire. The white men were dismounted . . . one man was left behind to take care of four horses, as the custom in dismounted fighting on the frontier. The camp was in the wildest commotion and women and children shrieked with terror. More than half the men were absent after the pony herd . . .

" 'The man who led those troops must have been drunk or crazy. He had the camp at his mercy, and could have killed us all or driven us away naked on the prairie. I don't believe there was a shot fired when his men commenced to retreat.' (Her husband qualified this by saying, 'Not much firing by the Indians.') 'But when they began to run away they ran very fast, and dropped their guns and ammunition. Our braves were not surprised by this time, and killed a good many when they crossed the plain to the river, while they were fording and on the hill beyond. I saw boys pull men from their horses and kill them on the ground.'

"Several times over [she] repeated her disgust at the action of the whites and the only explanation she could give for the

62

retreat was that Reno saw, when he got into it, how large the Indian village was and was seized with a panic greater than that among the Indians themselves. That the [Indian panic] was very decided was proven by the fact that the warriors hurriedly returning with the quickly rounded up herds, met many fugitives from the camp and feared the worst on their own return.

"The Reno retreat and its consequent slaughter was scarcely ended before the blare of Custer's trumpets told the Sioux of his approach. But they were prepared for him. The men quickly crossed the river, and by hundreds galloped to his rear, out of range at first, but taking advantage of coulee and mound, soon hemming him in constantly narrowing circles. Mrs. [Spotted Horn Bull] mounted her pony and rode to the first bench behind her camp, where she could get a good view of the hills beyond. She saw the troops come up, dismount, each fourth man seize the bridles of three horses beside his own, the rest deploy and advance on the run toward the river. She saw the terrible effect of the withering fire which greeted the approach from the willows on the Indian side of the stream, and laughed as she said: 'Our people, boys and all, had plenty of guns and ammunition to kill the new soldiers. Those who ran away [Reno's troopers] left them behind.'

"Slowly trotting north, along the outskirts of the encampment, she noted the Indians, who had crossed, getting closer to the troops. She watched the troops — those who were left of them — retreat to their horses and mount; she heard the yells of her kindred and the shouts of the whites; but soon, as the former grew plentier and the latter fewer, she could distinguish little, save here and there an animated cluster of men and horses. Slowly her pony jogged down the stream, and she reached the Minneconjou camp on the extreme left — not an hour's ride — she said not one white soldier was visible on the field. Of horses there were plenty. These the Indians spared, of course . . . they were fat and good looking, but (making a slow motion up and down with both hands) could only canter slowly, while the Indian ponies, 'like birds,' flitted in and through and about the troopers' broken

63

lines. Less than fifty minutes and more than five lives to the minute!

"From the husband was learned one incident of the day. One man, he thought an officer, was the last to live. He was mounted on a splendid horse (the color was forgotten), and seeing all his comrades dead, started up a ravine . . . Two Ogallalas, two Uncpapas and a Brule, all well mounted, started after him. He gained on them all, and one by one [they] dropped off until the Uncpapa, who was unarmed, as it turned out, alone pursued. The latter was about to give up the chase, when the soldier turned, saw his pursuer, noted that his own horse was flagging, drew a revolver from the holster at his hip and blew his own brains out.

" 'He had a good horse,' concluded her husband, 'And the Sioux [warrior] rode him for years after that.'

"The Sioux thought the distance ridden by pursuer and pursued was about seven miles from the battlefield, but it might have been more. Lieutenant Harrington's body was never found, or at least never recognized, and this sad suicide might have been he.

"Custer and his command killed, the Sioux again turned their attention to the troops on the hill and the woman, resuming the story, laughed gleefully as she told what fun the bucks had shooting at the soldiers as they ran that terrible gauntlet, down the hill to the river, for water . . . The Sioux lost thirty killed and more than twice as many wounded. Among the killed were boys of twelve and fourteen, who, in the ardor of young warriorhood, rushed across the river on their ponies and into the thickest of the fight. She mentioned two boys who were wounded; one, . . . in the heel, and another in the right arm, which was shot off. Both recovered and neither of them are yet twenty, though seven years have passed since they counted their first coups. It was with a tone of most noticeable regret that the woman told of the quantities of bank notes found and wasted, being utterly ignorant of the value of the curiously painted parallelograms of green paper.[3] She naively said: 'We know better about them now, and wouldn't lose them as we did at that time.'

64

"Of course, feasting and laudation was the order of the day and night succeeding the slaughter, but the news of Terry's approach with his command compelled a hasty breaking up of the camp. She says they marched day and night for several days, and soon the whole band was safe in the vastnesses of the Big Horn Mountains, where they remained some time before a separation took place, and the Uncpapas and portions of other tribes went north. The squaw's story was told straight-forwardly and beyond question she believes it true, every word. Neither she nor her husband had the slightest idea the account was to be published, and the appearance of a pencil and note book would have been the signal for a sudden cessation of the flow of conversation . . . To the question whether the bodies of the Custer command were much mutilated, the woman said, almost angrily, 'He-ya! He-ya! (No! No!) but afterward acknowledged that a good many scalps were taken."

Chapter Eight

On Custer Hill

*"We dance round in a ring and suppose,/
But the Secret sits in the middle and knows."*
Robert Frost

Lt. Colonel George A. Custer and the remaining five companies (C, E, F, I and L) had turned to the right and disappeared from the view of Major Reno's battalion who had just crossed the Little Big Horn River and were preparing to attack the village.

Although Custer did not discuss with his officers the details of his plan of attack, it is reasonably certain that he was heading downstream to attack the flank of the Indian village.

With Custer, as guides, were half-blood Sioux Indian interpreter Mitch Bouyer[1] and the four Crow scouts Curley, Hairy Moccasin, White-Man-Runs-Him and Goes Ahead.[2] Bouyer was killed but his advice, "to leave the fighting to the soldiers, watch from the hills and if we are getting licked make your way back to Terry and tell him we are all killed," saved the four Crow scouts. These scouts were familiar with the terrain and should have told Custer that the best place to descend the high bluff, cross the river and attack the village would be down Medicine Tail Coulee.

Custer's route to Medicine Tail Coulee passed closely by the hilltop where Reno would soon make his desperate fight for survival. At some point along the trail Custer left the column, which was riding on the eastern side of the bluffs out of sight of the village, and with Lt. W. W. Cooke and Trumpeter

Martin rode to the edge of the bluffs to get his first good look at his target. It was at this point that Lt. Charles A. Varnum and interpreter Fred Girard, who were in the valley with Reno, both swore they saw soldiers appear on the bluffs with Girard identifying Custer by sight.

"Custer . . . rode to the edge of the bluffs to get his first good look at his target."
Courtesy of John Willard

After leaving this vantage point Custer re-joined the column and proceeded about a mile farther towards the ridge where he would shortly lose his life. Halting the column at about the head of Medicine Tail Coulee, Custer had at his disposal the following information: 1.) Reno was in trouble. Captain Myles Keogh of Company I and Lt. W. W. Cooke, who had ridden a short distance with Reno's battalion before re-joining their own outfit, had undoubtedly relayed Fred Girard's message that the Indians were not fleeing, but were, in fact, coming up to meet the soldiers. Reno's messengers, McIlhargy and Mitchell, had reached Custer with basically

the same message. 2.) The village was immense, far bigg_.
than anyone expected.

It is probably at this point that Custer formulated his plan
of action. Whatever his plan and whatever his reasons for the
plan shall never be known because all who shared Custer's
final decisions would die with him within the next two hours.

Custer gave some verbal orders to Trumpeter John Martin
and instructed Martin to tell Benteen to come quick with the
ammunition packs. Lt. W. W. Cooke wrote these orders out
for Martin and handed them to him. The last Martin saw of
Custer and the five companies they were galloping down the
ravine with the Gray Horse Company (E) in the center.

The Indian accounts of the fight differ as to whether Custer
and his command actually reached the Little Big Horn River
and if they, in fact, attacked the village. Because of the
radically conflicting stories told later by the Indians it is quite
possible that the following or something similar to the
following happened that Sunday afternoon.

Custer, hoping to relieve the pressure on Reno, sent a
company down Medicine Tail Coulee in an attempt to create
a diversion and cause panic in the village, while Custer, with
the remaining companies, retired to a ridge east of the river
to provide a covering fire and await the arrival of Captain
Benteen and the pack train.

The Indians, superbly led by Gall and Crazy Horse, were
not surprised by the presence of Custer's command and had
been aware of it for some time; however, Reno's attack
caught them unaware and Gall and his followers turned to
meet Reno.

When Gall learned that the Custer soldiers were approaching the village at Medicine Tail Coulee opposite the camp of
the Minneconjou Sioux he left Reno's soldiers, who were now
reaching their hilltop position and therefore presented no
longer a threat to the Indians, and returned downstream to
meet this new threat.

The Crow scout Curley, the much publicized "only
survivor," later said that at about this time the Gray Horse
Company (E) left the command and started down the coulee

68

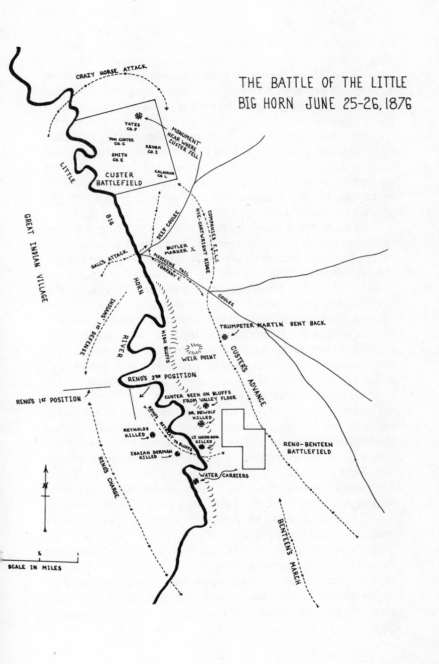

THE BATTLE OF THE LITTLE
BIG HORN JUNE 25-26,1876

CRAZY HORSE ATTACK

YATES
CO. F

TOM CUSTER
CO. C

KEOGH
CO. I

SMITH
CO. E

CUSTER
BATTLEFIELD

CALHOUN
CO. L

MONUMENT
NEAR WHERE
CUSTER FELL

LITTLE

BIG

DEEP COULEE

COMPANIES F,E,I,L,C
NYE-CARTWRIGHT RIDGE

GALL'S ATTACK

BUTLER
MARKER X

MEDICINE TAIL

COMPANY C

HORN

COULEE

GREAT INDIAN VILLAGE

INDIANS IN DEFENSE

RIVER

HIGH BLUFFS

WEIR POINT

TRUMPETER MARTIN SENT BACK

CUSTER'S ADVANCE

RENO'S 2ND POSITION

CUSTER SEEN ON BLUFFS
FROM VALLEY FLOOR

RENO'S 1ST POSITION

DR. DeWOLF
KILLED

RENO'S RETREAT TO BLUFFS

REYNOLDS
KILLED

LT. HODGSON
KILLED

RENO-BENTEEN
BATTLEFIELD

ISAIAH DORMAN
KILLED

RENO'S CHARGE

WATER CARRIERS

N

BENTEEN'S MARCH

SCALE IN MILES

towards the river while the rest of the column proceeded to the hills north of Medicine Tail Coulee. Curley, like the other three Crow Indian scouts on Mitch Bouyer's wise advice, left the column and thereby lived to tell of the soldiers' actions during the opening stages of the battle on the Custer portion of the battlefield.

Curley, separated from the other scouts, rode to a high ridge about one and a half miles east of the battlefield and watched until he was satisfied that what Mitch Bouyer had predicted would come to pass, then rode in the direction in which he thought General Terry, Colonel Gibbon and the Montana Column would be found.

Curley never did claim to be with Custer during the final frantic moments of the fight and the stories of his last minute escape from the jaws of death are purely the product of highly imaginative reporters.

The Gray Horse Company (E) was met near Medicine Tail crossing and some kind of action occurred in which the soldiers probably took some casualties. The fact that no soldier bodies were found near the ford could possibly be explained that early in the battle the soldiers carried their dead and wounded with them or that the bodies found later in the village could have been dragged from the ford.

At any rate, the soldiers were chased, probably by Gall and his followers, back in the direction of the ridge where Custer and the rest of the command were heading to wait for Benteen and the packs. This ridge, discovered in the 1920's by Joseph A. Blummer and largely neglected by Custer battle historians, was the scene of an action by the soldiers as over 600 cartridge shells have been found there. Cartridge cases were found later by R. G. Cartwright and Colonel Wilbur S. Nye. The ridge is now called the Nye-Cartwright ridge named after these men.

Crazy Horse, analyzing the situation, saw Gall repulse the Gray Horse Company near the river crossing, and, knowing of the presence of Custer's other four companies, led his followers downstream on the western side of the Little Big Horn River, crossed the river and circled around the northern

70

end of the battlefield thereby encircling the Custer command.

As Custer made his way to the Nye-Cartwright Ridge his view of Medicine Tail Ford was obstructed by intervening ridges and he could not see the fate that befell Company E as the Gray Horse Troop neared the river crossing. When Custer saw the large dust cloud rising from the floor of the valley he might have interpreted it to mean that the village was in flight when in fact the dust cloud was caused by Crazy Horse and his followers heading downstream in an effort to encircle Custer.

If Custer followed the natural contour of the land he would have approached the Nye-Cartwright Ridge from a south-easternly direction. Cresting the ridge he may have paused hoping that Trumpeter Martin had found Benteen and that reinforcements would be quickly coming. Seeing the rising dust cloud in the valley and fearing the Indians were escaping it is possible it was at this time he tried to attract Benteen's attention by firing the "distinct volleys" that were heard by various members of Reno's and Benteen's command.

Assuming three volleys were fired and Custer's command, less Company E, equalled about 180 men and if each man fired three bullets, this would account for the number of cartridge cases found on the Nye-Cartwright Ridge. The fact that the shells were found in a relatively straight line and no bodies were found within a half mile of the ridge indicates to this writer that not much, if any, pressure was being applied at this time to Custer's men by the Indians.

Custer, impatient with Benteen's failure to appear, elected to proceed without Benteen's additional three companies. If, in fact, this is the way it happened, Custer would have mounted his four companies and rode northward to stop, what he thought was, the fleeing village. Reaching a hog back ridge about a half mile north of the Nye-Cartwright Ridge, Custer could see the truth for the first time.

The Gray Horse Company (E) was straggling up from the river in disarray with Gall's warriors hotly in pursuit. The village was not in flight, in fact, Crazy Horse was crossing the river and would shortly encircle the northern end of the

After the Battle, *from "Treasures of the West"*
collection, courtesy of Mrs. Don C. Foote and
John E. Foote, Billings, Montana

battlefield. With no other choice, Custer was forced to make his last desperate stand on this long narrow ridge that overlooked the valley of the Little Big Horn River.

The Indian stories, gathered years later by enterprising reporters, told mostly of the individual Indian experiences during the battle and reflected only the events in which that particular Indian participated.

"With no other choice, Custer was forced to make his last desperate stand . . ."
Courtesy, Chamber of Commerce, Billings, Montana

On July 30, 1881 at Fort Yates, Dakota, about ninety miles down the Missouri River from Bismarck, a conference was held to discuss transferring recently surrendered Indians from the responsibility of the military to the Interior Department. Present at this conference were many of the Indian Chiefs who were present at the Battle of the Little Big Horn in 1876. An unknown reporter from the Leavenworth (Kansas) Weekly Times took the opportunity to interview a number of these chiefs. From that newspaper, published on August 18, 1881, these accounts of Ogalalla Chief Low Dog, Uncpapa Chief Crow King, Minneconjou Chief Hump and Iron Thunder appeared.

Low Dog's Account of the Custer Fight

" 'We were in camp near Little Big Horn River. We had lost some horses, and an Indian went back on the trail to look for them. We did not know that the white warriors were coming after us. Some scouts or men in advance of the warriors saw the Indian looking for the horses and ran after him and tried to kill him to keep him from bringing us word, but he ran faster than they and came into camp and told us that the white warriors were coming. I was asleep in my lodge at the time. The sun was about noon (pointing with his finger). I heard the alarm, but did not believe it. I thought it was a false alarm. I did not think it possible that any white men would attack us, so strong as we were. We had in camp the Cheyennes, Arapahoes, and seven different tribes of the Sioux — a countless number. Although I did not believe it was a true alarm, I lost no time getting ready. When I got my gun and came out of my lodge the [Reno] attack had begun at the end of the camp where Sitting Bull and the Uncpapas were. The Indians held their ground to give the women and children time to get out of the way. By this time the herders were driving the horses and as I was nearly at the further end of the camp, I ordered my men to catch their horses and get out of the way, and my men were hurrying to go and help those that were fighting. When the fighters saw that the women and children were safe they fell back. By this time my people went to help them, and the less able warriors and the women caught horses and got them ready, and we drove the first attacking party back, and that party retreated to a high hill. Then I told my people not to venture too far in pursuit for fear of falling into an ambush. By this time all the warriors in our camp were mounted and ready for fight, and then we were attacked on the other side by another party [Custer's command]. They came on us like a thunderbolt. I never before nor since saw men so brave and fearless as those white warriors. We retreated until our men got all together, and then we charged upon them. I called to my men, "This is a good day to die; follow me." We massed our men, and that no man should fall back, every man whipped another man's horse and we rushed right upon them. As we rushed upon them the white warriors dismounted to fire, but they did very poor shooting. They held their horses reins on one arm while they were shooting, but their horses were so frightened that they pulled the men all around, and a great many of their shots went up in the air and did us no harm. The white warriors stood their ground bravely, and none of them made any attempt to get away. After all but two of them were killed, I captured two of their horses. Then the wise men and chiefs of our nation gave out to our people not to mutilate the dead white chief, for he was a brave warrior and died a brave man, and his remains should be respected.

" 'Then I turned around and went to help fight the other white warriors, who had retreated to a high hill on the east side of the river. (This was Reno's command.) I don't know whether any white men of Custer's force were taken prisoners. When I got back to our camp they were all dead. Everything was in confusion all the time of the fight. I did not see General Custer. I do not know who killed him. We did not know till the fight was over that he was the white chief. We had no idea that the white warriors were coming until the runner came in and told us. I do not say that Reno was a coward. He fought well, but our men were fighting to save their women and children, and drive them back. If Reno and his warriors had fought as Custer and his warriors fought, the battle might have been against us. No white man or Indian ever fought as bravely as Custer and his men. The next day we fought Reno and his forces again, and killed many of them. Then the chiefs said these men had been punished enough, and that we ought to be merciful, and let them go. Then we heard that another force was coming up the river to fight us (General Terry's command,) and we started to fight them, but the chiefs and wise men counseled that we had fought enough and that we should not fight unless attacked, and we went back and took our women and children and went away.' "

"This ended Low Dog's narration, given in the hearing of half a dozen officers, some of the Seventeenth Infantry and some of the Seventh Cavalry — Custer's regiment. It was in the evening; the sun had set and the twilight was deepening. Officers were there who were at the Big Horn with Benteen, senior captain of the Seventh, who usually exercised command as a field officer, and who, with his battalion, joined Reno on the first day of the fight, after his retreat, and was in the second day's fight. It was a strange and intensely interesting scene. When Low Dog began his narrative only Captain [Henry Smith] Howe, the interpreter, and myself were present, but as he progressed the officers gathered round, listening to every word, and all were impressed that the Indian Chief was giving a true account, according to his knowledge. Someone asked how many Indians were killed in the fight, Low Dog answered, 'Thirty-eight, who died then, and a great many — I can't tell the number — who were wounded and died afterwards. I never saw a fight in which so many in proportion to the killed were wounded.' Another asked who were the dead Indians that were found in two tepees — five in one and six in the other — all richly dressed, and with their ponies, slain about the tepees. He said eight were chiefs killed in the battle. One was his own brother, born of the same mother and the same father, and he did not know who the other two were.

"The question was asked, 'What part did Sitting Bull take

77

in the fight?' Low Dog is not friendly to Sitting Bull. He answered with a sneer: 'If someone would lend him a heart he would fight.' Then Low Dog said he would like to go home, and with the interpreter he went back to the Indian camp. He is a tall, straight Indian, thirty-four years old, not a bad face, regular features and small hands and feet. He said that when he had his weapons and was on the war-path he considered no man his superior; but when he surrendered he laid that feeling all aside, and now if any man should try to chastise him in his humble condition and helplessness all he could do would be to tell him that he was no man and a coward; which, while he was on the warpath he could allow no man to say and live.''

Crow King's Story of the Fight

" 'We were in camp and not thinking there was any danger of a battle, although we had heard that the long-haired chief had been sent after us. Some of our runners went back and reported that an army of white soldiers was coming, and he had no more than reported when another runner came in with the same story, and also told us that the command had divided, and that one party [Custer] was going round to attack us on the opposite side.

" 'The first attack was at the camp of the Uncpapa tribe. The shots neither raised nor fell. (Here he indicated that the whites commenced firing at about four hundred yards distance.) The Indians retreated — at first slowly, to give the women and children time to go to a place of safety. Other Indians got our horses. By that time we had warriors enough to turn upon the whites and we drove them to the hill, and started back to camp.

" 'Then the second band of white warriors came. We did not know who was their chief, but we supposed it was Custer's command. The party commenced firing at long range. (Indicating nearly a mile.) We had then all our warriors and horses. There were eight warriors in my band. All the Sioux were there from everywhere. We had warriors plenty as the leaves on the trees. Our camp was as long as from the fort to the lower end of our camp here. (More than two and a half miles.) Sitting Bull and Crazy Horse were the great chiefs of the fight. Sitting Bull did not fight himself, but he gave orders. We turned against this second party [Custer]. The greater portion of our warriors came together in their front and we rushed our horses on them. At the same time warriors rode out on each side of them and circled around them until they were surrounded. When they saw that they were surrounded they dismounted. They tried to hold on to their horses, but as we pressed closer they let go their horses. We crowded them toward our main camp and killed them all. They kept in order and fought like brave warriors as long as they had a man left. Our camp was on Greasy Grass river, (Little Big Horn). When we charged every chief gave

". . . but as we pressed closer they let go their horses."

the cry, 'Hi-yi-yi.' (Here Crow King gave us the cry in a high, prolonged tone.)

" 'When this cry is given it is a command to all the warriors to watch the chief, and follow his actions. Then every chief rushed his horse on the white soldiers, and all our warriors did the same, every one whipping another's horse. There was great hurry and confusion in the fight. No one chief was above another in that fight. It was not more than half an hour after the long-haired chief attacked us before he and all his men were dead.

" 'Then we went back for the first party [Reno]. We fired at them until the sun went down. We surrounded them and watched them all night, and at daylight we fought them again. We killed many of them. Then a chief from the Uncpapas called our men off. He told them those men had been punished enough, that they were fighting under orders, that we had killed the great leader and his men in the fight the day before, and we should let the rest go home. Sitting Bull gave this order. He said, "This is not my doings, nor these men's. They are fighting because they were commanded to fight. We have killed their leader. Let them go. I call on the Great Spirit to witness what I say. We did not want to fight. Long Hair sent us word that he was coming to fight us, and we had decided to defend ourselves and our wives and children." If this command had not been given we could have cut Reno's command to pieces, as we did Custer's. No warrior knew Custer in the fight. We did not know him, dead or alive. When the fight was over the chiefs gave orders to look for the long-haired chief among the dead, but no chief with long hair could be found.' (Custer had his hair cut short before starting on this march.)

"Crow King said that if Reno had held out until Custer came and then fought as Custer did, that they would have whipped the Indians. The Indians would then have been compelled to divide to protect their women and children, and the whites would have had the advantage. He expressed great admiration for the bravery of Custer and his men, and said that that fight impressed the Indians that the whites were

80

their superiors and it would be their destruction to keep on fighting them. Both he and Low Dog said that they did not feel that they would be blamed for the Custer fight or its results. It was war; they were attacked; Custer tried to kill them; they killed him.

"Crow King said he had two brothers killed in the fight; that from thirty to fifty Indians were killed, and a much larger number, who were wounded, died afterward."

Hump's Story of the Custer Fight

"The sun was about at meridian when the fight began. (This he indicated by pointing; the Indians have no division of time corresponding to our hours.) That was the first we knew that the white warriors were coming. They attacked the Uncpapas first. They were at the upper end of our camp. The Minneconjous, Sans-Arcs and Cheyennes were near the center of the camp, but nearer the end of the camp furthest from where the attack was made. The charge was from the upper end of the camp. The Indians gave way slowly, retreating until they got their horses and got mounted. Just as soon as they got sufficient force — for our warriors were rushing to help them as fast as they could — they drove the white warriors back, and they retreated. These were Reno's men. I had a horse that I could not manage. He was not mine, and was not well broke; so I went to where the horses were, and the women and the old men and boys were gathering them together, and caught a horse that I could manage better, and when I had caught him and mounted, the other party of white warriors (Custer's forces) charged. The Indians had by that time all got together, and it seemed, the way Custer came, that he started to cut off our retreat, not appearing to know where Reno was, or that he had retreated. When the Indians charged on the long-haired chief and his men, the long-haired chief and his men became confused, and they retreated slowly, but it was no time at all before the Indians had the long-haired chief and his men surrounded. Then our chiefs gave the 'Hi-yi-yi' yell, and all the Indians

"It was no time at all before the Indians had the long haired chief and his men surrounded."

joined, and they whipped each other's horses, and they made such short work of killing them, that no man could give any correct account of it. The Indians and whites were so mixed up that you could hardly tell anything about it.

"The first dash the Indians made my horse was shot from under me and I was wounded — shot above the knee, and the ball came out at the hip (here the interpreter said that he had seen the scar), and I fell and lay right there. The rest of the Indians kept on horseback, and I did not get in the final fight. It was a clear day. There was no storm nor thunder nor lightning. The report was that it was the long-haired chief that came to fight us, but that was all that we knew.

"I know that Sitting Bull was in the fight, but on account of my wound I did not know anything he did. Every able-bodied Indian there took part in the fight, as far as I could tell. Those that did not join in the fight it was because they could not find room to get in. There were a good many agency Indians in our camp. They all took part in the fight, same as the hostiles. The agency Indians had come out, and all made report to us that Long-Hair was coming to fight us. So the Indians all got together that he might not strike small parties, and not for the purpose of fighting or counciling with Long-Hair . . . but they were getting ready to be strong to defend themselves.

82

Iron Thunder's Story

"We were encamped on the west side of the Little Big Horn. On the upper side of the camp was a small ash grove more than two miles down the river. The tepees were close together, one band adjoining another all the way down. I did not know anything about Reno's attack until his men were so close that the bullets went through the camp, and everything was in confusion. The horses were so frightened we could not catch them. I was catching my horse to join the fight. When I caught him and was mounted, our warriors had driven the white men off and were running after them. Then I followed the way they went, and I saw a lot of horsemen — Indians — crossing the river, and went after them. I followed them across the river, and before I overtook them, going up the hill, I found an Indian lying there dead. I knew him. He and I were sworn friends. I stopped to look at him. The whites were still firing back at us. Just as I arrived where our men were, the report came to us that another party [Custer] was coming to attack us. We could not see them from where we were. The report was that they were coming to head off the women and children from the way they were going, and so we turned around and went towards them. Our men moved around in the direction of a circle, but I cut across the knoll and looked up the river and saw them coming down. The day before the fight I had come back from a war party against the Crows. I had only one horse, and his feet were worn out (the Indians do not shoe their horses, and they often give out on long marches), and by the time I got half-way back to where Long-Haired Chief and his men were my horse was so lame I could go no further. I was nearly two miles away when the Indians charged the Long-Haired Chief and his warriors. You could not notice the difference in the sun from the time when Custer was charged until he was done away with. Agency Indians, Yanktons and Santees were there. All took part. Every Indian took part in the fight that could, but there was such confusion that no one could tell the particulars of what was done."

Chapter Nine

After the Battle

After Custer's command left the mouth of Rosebud Creek on June 22 and marched south following the Indian trail that would lead to the valley of the Little Big Horn, General Terry with Colonel Gibbon and the Montana column proceeded to carry out their part of the campaign.

Under the overall command of General Terry the six companies of the Seventh Infantry, four companies of Major Brisbin's Second Cavalry, the 25 Crow Indian Scouts under the command of Lieutenant James Bradley and the detachment of Gatling guns under the command of Lieutenant Charles A. Woodruff, a total of about 450 men, were to head west up the Yellowstone River to the mouth of the Big Horn River, follow that river upstream to the mouth of the Little Big Horn River, where the column would turn left or east and follow that river towards the valley of the Little Big Horn where the Indians were expected to be found. Terry was hoping that the Indians would be found between Custer's Seventh Cavalry coming from the opposite direction and his column coming up the Little Big Horn River.

The accounts available of this march up the Big Horn by the Montana column reveal the difficulties encountered and hardships suffered by these troops. Night marches over terrain that was badly cut up by deep ravines and gullies caused the outfit to lose their way and made their progress slow and difficult.

The troops, especially the infantry, were exhausted but little time was available for adequate rest and food. It seems that everyone, not just Custer, was obsessed with the thought that the Indians would flee before a military action could be initiated.

On the 25th, while Custer was being wiped out, the Montana column was, as Lieutenant Bradley wrote, "involved in a labyrinth of bald hills and deep, precipitous ravines completely destitude of water."

The following day Lieutenant Bradley and his Crow Indian scouts encountered White-Man-Runs-Him. Hairy Moccasin and Goes Ahead, three of the four Crow scouts that, on the advice of Mitch Bouyer, had left Custer during the early stages of the battle. Curley did not appear until later.

It was here that the news of Custer's disaster was first learned but was not wholly accepted by the officers of the Montana column when Bradley rushed back to report this news. The Crow scouts believed the news was beyond dispute as they, very shortly, galloped away together and rode back to the agency from whence they had been recruited in April.

Terry had no choice but to continue on in the direction he was heading and find out for sure what had happened. Indians had been sighted observing the column as it made its way down the valley and attempts were made by the Sioux to lure these new troops into an ambush. The column made camp on the night of June 26 at the place where present day Crow Agency is located.

Colonel John Gibbon, in an article that appeared in the American Catholic Quarterly Review in April and October of 1877 wrote of what his column discovered when dawn broke the following day over the valley of the Little Big Horn.

". . . Everyone was astir at the first appearance of day, and after a hurried breakfast of hardtack, bacon, and coffee, the march was resumed up the valley . . . we caught sight, through the scattered timber, of a couple of Indian tepees standing in the open valley . . . At length we reached the tepees, found them occupied by dead Indians laid out in state, and surrounded in every direction with the remnants and various odds and ends of a hastily abandoned camp. Tepee poles, skins, robes, pots, kettles, and pans lay scattered in every direction. But we had little time or inclination to comment on these sights, for every thought was now bent upon the possible fate of our fellow-soldiers, and the desire was intense to solve as soon as possible the dread doubt which now began to fill our minds. For, in searching about amongst the rubbish, someone had picked up a pair of bloody drawers, upon which was plainly written the words, 'Sturgis - 7th Cavalry,' whilst a buckskin shirt recognized as belonging to Lieutenant Porter, was discovered with a bullet-hole passing through it.[1]

". . . Looking up the valley I caught sight of something on the top of a hill . . . which at once attracted my attention and a closer scrutiny. I sprang from my horse, and with a field glass looked long and anxiously at a number of dark objects which might be either animals or stubby cedar trees . . . One of General Terry's staff officers took the glass and seating himself on the ground peered long and anxiously at the spots, but finally said, 'they are not animals.'[2] But scarcely had the words escaped him, when we both noticed a very apparent increase in the number of objects on the highest point of the hill, and now one doubt was solved only to give rise to another. Were the objects seen friends or foes?

". . . Whilst watching these lookouts and wondering at their strange movements, the officer in charge of the mounted infantry party,[3] in the hills to the north of us, rode up to where General Terry and I sat upon our horses, and his voice trembled as he said, 'I have a very sad report to make. I have counted one hundred and ninety-seven dead bodies lying in the hills!' 'White men?' was the first question asked. 'Yes, white men.' A look of horror was upon every face, and for a moment no one spoke. There could be no question now. The Crows were right, and Custer had met with a disaster, but the extent of it was still a matter of doubt; . . . From out of the timber near the point, a horseman at full speed was now seen coming towards us. It was my staff officer coming with news, and as he approached us on the full run he called out, 'I have seen scouts from Major Reno, who report their regiment cut to pieces, and . . . Major Reno fortified in the bluffs with the remnant.' . . . After we had gone about a mile a party of horsemen was seen approaching, and as we rode forward to meet them we recognized two young officers of the Seventh Cavalry,[4] followed by several orderlies. Hands were grasped almost in silence, but we questioned eagerly with our eyes, and one of the first things they uttered was, 'Is General Custer with you?' On being told that we had not seen him, they gave us hurriedly an account of the operations of the past two days, and the facts began to dawn upon us. No one of the party which accompanied General Custer when the command was divided, about noon on the 25th, had been seen by the survivors, and our inference was, that they were all, or nearly all, lying up in the hills where our scouting party had found the dead bodies.

"Comanche, Captain Myles Keogh's horse, was discovered badly wounded on Custer ridge."

". . . Nearly the whole valley was black and smoking with the fire which had swept over it, and it was with some difficulty I could find grass sufficient for our animals, as it existed only in spots close to the stream where too green to burn. Except for the fire, the ground presented but few evidences of the conflict which had taken place. Now and then a dead horse was seen; but as I approached a bend of the creek (for it is little more than a creek), just below the hill occupied by the troops, I came upon the body of a soldier lying on his face near a dead horse. He was stripped, his scalp gone, his head beaten in, and his body filled with bullet-holes and arrows. Close by was another body, also close to a dead horse, lying, like the other, on its face, but partially clothed, and this was recognized by one of our officers as the body of . . . Lt. McIntosh. More bodies of both men and horses were found close by, and it was noted that the bodies of men and horses laid almost always *in pairs,* and as this was the ground over which Major Reno's command retired towards the hills after its charge down the valley, the inference was drawn, that in the run the horses must have been killed first, and the riders after they fell.

". . . Looking down the river in the direction we had come was a point of timber jutting out into the plain, where for a portion of the time the cavalry had fought dismounted; and beyond this, in plain sight from where I stood, was located the village where the fight began; and opposite that, hidden from sight by the high peak so often referred to,[5] was the scene of Custer's fight, where his body was found surrounded by those of his men and horses.

"On the highest point of the ridge occupied by the Reno troops, and along what had been the northern line of defence, were pitched a number of shelter tents, and under and about these were lying some fifty wounded men, receiving the care of the surgeons and their attendants. The cheerfulness of these poor fellows under their sufferings, and their evident joy at their rescue was touching in the extreme, and we listened with full hearts to their recital in feeble tones of the long anxious hours of waiting and fighting during which every eye

88

was strained, looking for the coming succor, hoping for its arrival, yet fearing it would be too late. At one time, so strongly did the imagination affect the judgment, the whole command was convinced that columns of troops could be seen moving over the hills to their assistance, but in directly the *opposite* direction from which they actually came. So strong was this delusion that the buglers of the whole command were assembled and ordered to sound their bugles to attract attention. When we finally made our appearance down the valley, the same thing was done, and it is supposed that it was the gathering together of the buglers on the highest point of the hill which finally decided in our minds that we were looking at men and horses, and not clumps of cedar trees. But we heard nothing of the bugles, for the wind was blowing from us.

"Now and then a dead horse was seen . . ."

". . . One of Major Reno's companies is mounted and started for the scene of Custer's fight.[6] It leaves our position, and winding along the rolling hills, ascends the high ground to the right of the high peak, and disappears beyond, just as Custer's command would have vanished probably from the sight of an observer standing where we are now.

"Whilst this company is away we are busy preparing to remove the wounded down from the hot, dusty hill where they are lying to my camp, where they will be more comfortable and can be better cared for.

"After being absent a couple of hours the detached company is seen winding its way back, and as it approaches we all collect round General Terry to hear the report of its gray-haired captain,[7] who won such praises by his indomitable bearing in the fight. He comes forward, dismounts, and in a low, very quiet voice, tells his story. He had followed Custer's trail to the scene of the battle opposite the main body of the Indian camp, and amid the rolling hills which borders the river-bank on the north. As he approached the ground scattered bodies of men and horses were found, growing more numerous as he advanced. In the midst of the field a long *backbone* ran out obliquely back from the river, rising very gradually until it terminated in a little knoll which commanded a view of all the surrounding ground, and of the Indian campground beyond the river. On each side of this backbone, and sometimes on top of it, dead men and horses were scattered along. These became more numerous as the terminating knoll was reached; and on the southwestern slope of that lay the brave Custer surrounded by the bodies of several of his officers and forty or fifty of his men, whilst horses were scattered about in every direction. All were stripped, and most of the bodies were scalped and mutilated. And now commenced the duty of recognizing the dead. Of Custer there could be no doubt. He was lying in a perfectly natural position as many had seen him lying when asleep, and, we were told, was not at all mutilated, and that, only after a good deal of search the wounds of which he died could be found. The field was searched and one after another the officers were found and and recognized, all except two.[8] A count of the bodies disclosed the fact that some twenty-five or thirty were missing, and we could not, until some time afterwards, form even a surmise in regard to their fate.[9]

"The great mystery was now solved, at last, of the destruction of that part of Custer's command. It was possible that some few individuals might have escaped the general massacre; but so far as we could judge all had fallen; and the particulars of that sad and desperate conflict against overwhelming numbers of the savage horde which flocked about Custer and his devoted three hundred[10] when Reno was beaten back, will never be known.

"The poor wounded claimed my first care. They were lying on the hot dusty hill under inadequate shelter, and steps were taken at once to remove them to my cooler, pleasanter camp on the creek-bank below. The majority of them had to be carried, and there was not a single stretcher or litter in the command. These had therefore to be improvised. A quantity of the light tepee poles were collected from the Indian camp, and by means of these, old pieces of canvas, and blankets, a number were made, and by night all of the wounded were carried down the steep slope of the bluffs, across the creek, and down to our camp, the men working by relays.

"The Seventh Cavalry remained upon the bluffs during the night, and early the next morning moved down to the scene of Custer's conflict, to perform the mournful duty of burying the remains of their slaughtered comrades. This would have been an impracticable task but for the discovery, in the deserted Indian camp, of a large number of shovels and spades, by the aid of which the work was performed.

"The formidable question of the transportation of the wounded now came up and had to be met. The mouth of the Little Big Horn to which point the steamer 'Far West' had been ordered, was some twenty miles distant, and couriers had been dispatched to communicate with her, ascertain if she had reached there, and warn her to await our arrival. In the meantime, we set to work to construct the necessary litters with what rough material could be collected. Lieute-

"At first two men were assigned to each hand-litter . . ."

nant Gustavus C. Doane of the Second Cavalry volunteered to construct horse-litters out of rough cottonwood poles, rawhide, and ropes, but the process proved a very slow and tedious one, and other details were set to work collecting tepee poles and manufacturing hand-litters out of them and such old canvas as was to be had. Late in the afternoon, but four or five of the horse-litters had been finished, and the necessary number was completed with hand-litters. But on trying the mules in the horse-litters (all of them animals taken from baggage-wagons, unused to carrying packs, and sore from their few days' service under the saddles), most of them proved so refractory in the novel position assigned them, that grave doubts arose as to whether the suffering wounded could be safely carried in this way.

"It was to be feared that any show of precipitancy in leaving our position was calculated to invite an attack from the overwhelming number of our enemies, and we should probably not have started that day at all, but for the report of the surgeons that it was indispensable that the wounded should be removed at once to avoid the ill effects of the heat and the flies that swarmed around them in immense numbers from the dead bodies in the vicinity. It was therefore decided late in the afternoon to commence the movement, and as the sun sank behind the western hills, the wounded were transferred to the litters and the sad cortege moved out of camp.

"At first two men were assigned to each hand-litter, but it was soon found that this was not sufficient, and the number had to be doubled, and, besides, two men had to be assigned to each horse-litter to steady it. Infantrymen and dismounted cavalrymen relieved each other every few minutes, but our progress was slow and laborious, and before we had made more than a mile from our camp, darkness overtook our straggling and disorganized column, completely broken up by the repeated halts and constantly recurring changes of carriers.

"As we moved through the darkness, the silence of night broken only by the tramp of men and horses and the groans of the suffering wounded, I could not help contrasting the scene presented with that gay spectacle we had witnessed only six days before. When Custer's splendid regiment moved out in solid column, with its guidons fluttering in the breeze as it disappeared from our sight over the bluffs at the mouth of the Rosebud.

"Long, tedious, and slow, the hours of that sad night wore on, and it was past midnight before we reached camp at a distance of only four and a half miles.

". . . Our march of four and a half miles on the 28th demonstrated that it was practically out of the question to transport the wounded in anything like a reasonable time in the hand-litters, and, as the command laid over the next day for the purpose of destroying the large quantity of property left behind in the Indian camp, the delay was taken advantage of to construct, under the superintendence of Lieutenant Doane an additional number of mule-litters, the few he had made the day before having worked satisfactorily. Ash poles were obtained, several dead horses lying about the camp were skinned for rawhide, and by the afternoon nearly the requisite number was completed, the full number being made up by structures called 'travailles,' or 'travoirs,' in imitation of the Indian method. These consist of a couple of lodge poles, having one end fastened to the saddle of a packhorse, and the other trailing on the ground, the two being fastened together just behind the tail of the horse by a wicker-work platform, on which the patient reclines. The light flexible poles act as springs, and except over very rough ground, the movement is far from disagreeable or rough. All the animals of the pack-train were now picked over, and the most gentle and best broken of these were turned over to Lieutenant Doane for service with the litters.

"A number of companies were now sent out, scattered all over the site of the camp, to collect and destroy the property left by the Indians, and soon columns of smoke were seen rising in every direction from burning lodge-poles, upon which were thrown vast quantities of robes, dressed skins of different kinds, and other inflammable objects, while such

94

pans, kettles, cups, and *crockery,* as were not needed by the troops were broken up.

"Up to this time I had no opportunity to personally visit the scene of Custer's battle, and taking advantage of our delay in camp, which was situated just below and beyond the limits of the old Indian camp, I that morning rode up to the spot, and went over most of the ground.

". . . As we proceeded up the valley, now an open grassy slope, we suddenly came upon a body lying in the grass. It was lying upon its back and was in an advanced state of decomposition. It was not stripped, but had evidently been scalped and one ear cut off. The clothing was not that of a soldier, and, with the idea of identifying the remains, I caused one of the boots to be cut off and the stocking and drawers examined for a name, but none could be found. On looking at the boot, however, a curious construction was observed. The heel of the boot was reinforced by a piece of leather which in front terminated in two straps, one of which was furnished with a buckle, evidently for the purpose of tightening the instep of the boot. This led to the identification of the remains, for on being carried to camp the boot was recognized as one belonging to Mr. [Mark] Kellogg, a newspaper correspondent who accompanied General Custer's column. Beyond this point the ground commenced to rise more rapidly, and the valley was broken up into several smaller ones which lead up towards the higher ground beyond. Following up one of these we reach a rolling but not very broken space, the ground rising higher and higher until it reaches a culminating knoll dominating all the ground in the immediate vicinity. This knoll, by common consent now called Custer's Hill, is the spot where his body was found surrounded by those of several of his officers and some forty or fifty of his men. We can see from where we are numerous bodies of dead horses scattered along its southwestern slope, and as we ride up towards it, we come across another body lying in a depression just as if killed whilst using his rifle there. We follow the sloping ground bearing a little to the left or westward until we reach the top, and then look around us.

On the very top are four or five dead horses, swollen, putrid, and offensive, their stiffened limbs sticking straight out from their bodies. On the slope beyond others are thickly lying in all conceivable positions, and dotted about on the ground in all directions are little mounds of freshly turned earth, showing where each brave soldier sleeps his last sleep. Close under the brow of the knoll several horses are lying nearer together than the rest, and by the side of one of these we are told the body of Custer was found. The top of the knoll is only a few feet higher than the general surface of the long straight ridge, which runs off obliquely towards the river, in the direction of that ford at which it is supposed Custer made the attempt to cross.

". . . Custer's Hill dominates over the whole surrounding country. Standing upon that he must have had a full view of the struggle taking place around him, and of the Indian village lying at his feet, but not within his power. And when forced back by overwhelming numbers, only to find the valley behind filled also with yelling hordes of savages, he must, whilst straining his eyes in that direction from which alone help could come,[11] have recognized when too late the courageous-born error he committed in dividing his force in the presence of so numerous an enemy.

"The body of our poor guide, Mitch Bouyer, was found lying in the midst of the troopers, slain, as the Sioux had several times reported they had slain him, in battle. He was a half-breed Sioux, and they had often tried to kill him. He was the protege and pupil of the celebrated guide Jim Bridger; was the best guide in this section of the country, and the only half-breed I ever met who could give the distances to be passed over with any accuracy *in miles* . . .

"By the burial-place of each officer was driven to the head a stake, in the top of which a hole was bored, and in this was placed a paper having upon it the name and rank of the officer.

"On leaving the battle-ground we bore obliquely to the right, and making our way over the steep bluffs down the river, near the mouth of the deep gulch mentioned as containing so many of our dead troopers, pushed our way through the brushwood of the riverbank, and, crossing the river at a shallow ford, entered the site of the Indian camp, where our working parties were still busy searching for, collecting, and destroying the Indian property, part of which was found concealed in the brush.

"Riding across the valley towards the bluffs, we passed the site of the two tepees filled with dead Indians, now a mass of charred remains, and approached a clump of small trees, in and near which the Indians had buried a number of their dead, the ponies slaughtered in their honor lying about the remains of their dead masters, now tumbled upon the ground from the destruction of the scaffolding by those human ghouls whose existence seems to be inseparable from a fighting force, *after* the fighting is over, and whose vandal acts painfully impress one with the conviction that in war barbarism stands upon a level only a little lower than our boasted modern civilization.

". . . Turning from this revolting spectacle, we rode back to camp to find the work of litter-making going on bravely and successfully. About the camp numerous mules in couples, between the rude shafts of the litters, were being led about to get accustomed to the awkward movement and under the direction of the indefatigable Lieutenant Doane the men as well as the mules were being instructed how to turn, how to advance, hold back, etc., so that the poor suffering burdens should neither be thrown out nor shaken more roughly than was necessary.

"At length all was ready; the wounded were lifted as tenderly as possible into the litters, and at six o'clock in the afternoon we started, expecting to make a short march, more to test the litters than anything else. But we had not gone more than a few miles and had just crossed the river a second time when two horsemen[12] made their appearance on the bluffs on our left, and our couriers rode into the column bringing us news that the 'Far West' was awaiting for us at the mouth of the Little Big Horn.

"Assured now of the close proximity of the boat, and

97

anxious to get the wounded as soon as possible within its comfortable shelter, General Terry decided to push forward at once for the mouth of the stream. The mule-litters were working beyond our most sanguine expectations, both as regarded comfort and rapidity of movement, and all felt that Lieutenant Doane, by his energy and skill, had relieved us from a difficult dilemma, and our wounded from prolonged suffering. We therefore pushed rapidly down the valley, keeping near the bluffs, for Bostwick informed us that we must mount these and cross a high, wide plateau,[13] before we could reach the boat.

"Comanche, Captain Myles Keogh's horse and the only living survivor of the Custer fight found on the battle-field, was placed on the deck of the Far West."
From **Rhymes of a Cowboy** *by J. K. Ralston*

". . . The column was now halted, and in company with a staff officer I rode forward to try and pick out a way. I was soon compelled to dismount, but we finally succeeded in making our way down to a lower level, and whilst going towards the light were hailed by a challenge. In answer to our call, 'Who are you?' came back the welcome words, 'Captain [Stephen] Baker, of the Sixth Infantry,' (the officer in charge of the boat), and in a few minutes he was mounted on my horse and on his way back to the head of the column, whilst I reached the boat and started men out to build fires along the route. They were all up and expecting us, on the boat; and the lower deck, inclosed with canvas, was prepared with beds to make our wounded as comfortable as possible." ("Messengers had reported that over half a hundred wounded were being borne down the valley from Reno's field. The crew and soldiers under Captains Marsh and Baker sprang to work with a will to prepare the steamer for their coming. The boilers of the *Far West* stood near the bow and between them and the stern was a wide, open space where Baker's men had made their quarters. This was turned into a hospital, and under the directions from Doctor Williams, the army surgeon on board, the floor was completely covered to a depth of eighteen inches with fresh grass cut from the low marsh lands along the river. When it had been spread, enough new tarpaulins were taken from the quartermaster's stores on board to carpet the whole deck like an immense mattress. Around the sides were arranged the medicine chests, ready for use. After all was completed, Doctor Williams declared it to be the best field hospital he had ever seen.")[14] "It was now long after midnight, the side of the hill was soon ablaze with a line of fires, and by the light of these the litters made their way down, and when dawn commenced to streak the eastern sky, our poor patient sufferers were comfortably at rest on the deck of the *Far West*.

"The next day she started down the river, . . ."

Chapter Ten

The Trip Back to Fort Lincoln
on the Steamer Far West

Of the three medical doctors that accompanied the Custer
column from the mouth of the Rosebud to the valley of the
Little Big Horn, only Dr. Henry R. Porter survived. Dr.
James M. DeWolf was killed by an Indian sharpshooter as
the doctor was ascending the bluffs while attempting to join
Reno in his hilltop position. Dr. George Edwin Lord was
killed with Custer and together with three 7th Cavalry officers
(Lt. James E. Porter, Lt. Henry M. Harrington and Lt. James
G. Sturgis) his body was never found.

Dr. Porter remained in the service following the Custer
fight and served with General George Crook in Arizona and
as post surgeon at Camp Hancock, Dakota Territory until his
retirement from army life in 1887.

Dr. Porter died on March 3, 1903 in Agra, British India
while on one of his global trips that he so thoroughly enjoyed
during his retirement years.

Porter, after narrowly escaping death in the valley with
Reno, served bravely and selflessly tending the wounded
during the fight on Reno Hill and afterwards accompanied
the casualties on the painful and laborious march to the
mouth of the Little Big Horn River where the steamboat *Far
West* was waiting. Dr. Porter told the story of the "lightning
steamboat ride" back to Fort Abraham Lincoln to his good
friend Clement A. Lounsberry, the editor of the *Bismarck
Tribune,* and the story was published in the February and
March 1897 issues of *The Record.* From the story we quote
portions that describe that remarkable steamboat ride.

"The steamer *Far West* was moored at the mouth of the Little Big Horn. She was the supply boat of the expedition and had made her way up the Big Horn farther than any other boat. She had performed one exploit unprecedented in western river navigation in reaching the mouth of the Little Big Horn, and was ready to perform another unequaled in steamboating in the west. The wounded were carried on board the steamer and Dr. Porter was detailed to go down with them.[1] Terry's adjutant general, Colonel Ed. [Capt. Edward W.] Smith, was sent along with the official dispatches and a hundred other messages. He had a traveling bag full of telegrams for the Bismarck office. Captain Grant Marsh was in command of the *Far West*. He put everything in the completest order and took on a large amount of fuel. He received orders to reach Bismarck as soon as possible. He understood his instructions literally, and never did a river man obey them more conscientiously. On the evening of the third of July the steamer weighed anchor. In a few minutes the *Far West*, so fittingly named, was under full head of steam. It was a strange land, and an unknown river. What a cargo on that steamer! What news for the country! What a story to carry to the government, to Fort Lincoln, to the widows!

"It was running from a field of havoc to a station of mourners. The steamer *Far West* never received the credit due her. Neither has the gallant Marsh. Nor the pilots David Campbell and John Johnson. Marsh, too, acted as pilot. It required all their endurance and skill. They proved the men of emergency. The engineer, whose name is not known to me, did his duty.[2] Every one of the crew is entitled to the same acknowledgement. They felt no sacrifice was too great upon that journey, and in behalf of the wounded heroes. A very moderate imagination can picture the scene upon that floating hospital.

"There were wounds of every character, and men more dead than alive. The suffering was not terminated with the removal from the field to the boiler deck. It continued and ended in death more than once before Fort Lincoln was hailed. Porter watched for fifty-four hours. He stood the test. The Big Horn is full of islands, and a successful passage, even on the bosom of a 'June rise' is not an easy feat. The *Far West* would take a shoot on this or that side of an island, as the quick judgment of the pilot would dictate . . . A steamboat moving as fast as a railway train in a narrow, winding stream is not a pleasure. It was no pleasant sensation to be dashing straight at a headland, and the pilot the only power to save. Occasionally the bank would be touched and the men would topple over like ten-pins. It was a reminder of what the result would be if a snag was struck. Down the Big Horn the heroine went, missing islands, snags and shore. It was a thrilling voyage. The rate of speed was unrivaled in the annals of boating. Into the Yellowstone the staunch craft shot, and down that sealed river . . . she made over twenty miles an hour. The bold captain was taking chances, but he scarcely thought of them. He was under flying orders. Lives were at stake. His engineer was instructed to keep up steam at the highest pitch. Once the steam gauge marked a pressure

". . . *the* Far West *was awaiting for us at the mouth of the Little Big Horn.*"
Courtesy, Big Horn County Bank, Hardin, Montana

that turned his cool head and made every nerve in his powerful frame quiver. The crisis passed and the *Far West* escaped a fate more terrible than Custer's. Once a stop was made and a shallow grave explained the reason. He still rests in that lonely spot.[3] Down the swift Yellowstone, . . . into the broad Missouri, and then there was clear sailing. There was a deeper channel and more confidence. A few minutes were lost at Fort Buford. Everybody at the fort was beside himself. The boat was crowded with inquirers, and their inquiries were not half answered when the steamer was away. At [Buford] a wounded scout[4] was put off, and at Fort Stevenson a brief stop to tell in a word what had happened.[5] There was no difference in the speed from Stevenson to Bismarck. The same desperate rate was kept up to the end. They were approaching home with something of that feeling which always moves the human heart. At 11 o'clock on the night of the 5th of July they reached Bismarck, and Fort Abraham Lincoln. One thousand miles in fifty-four hours was the proud record.[6] You have Captain Marsh's challenge to produce a duplicate.

"Dr. Porter and Colonel Smith hurried from the landing up town, calling up the editor of the [Bismarck] *Tribune* and the telegraph operator. The latter, J. M. Carnahan, took his seat at the key the next morning and scarce raised himself from his chair for twenty-two hours. He, too, was plucky, and what he sent vibrating around the world is history.

"What a night! Colonel Lounsberry was editor of the *Tribune* then . . . Porter, Smith, Fred Girard, Grant Marsh, and nearly a score of others were interviewed that night. A brief bulletin to the *New York Herald,* 'Custer and his whole command massacred. Not one left to tell the tale.' Terry gathered up the notes written by Mark Kellogg's hand, of the progress of the march up to the beginning of the battle.[7] General [Major] James S. Brisbin sent notes of the battlefield as he found it and saw it. These were filed. There was a column or two of Mark's work and two or more of Brisbin's. 'Take this,' said Lounsberry, as he handed Carnahan a copy of the *New Testament.* 'Fire that in when you run out of

103

copy. Hold the wires. Tell 'em it's coming and to hold the key!' With almost the speed of lightning flew the editor's hand . . . Porter, Girard, Marsh and others told their stories and they were put on the wires. The list of the dead, of those wounded, and the incidents in relation to each, were poured into his ears or brought the editor by willing hands. To sleep, or even tire under such circumstances was not likely. The story grew. Fifteen thousand words had gone and still there was more, and the story grew in interest. The wee small hours had gone and daylight came and still the keys were busy. What Custer said. What Custer did. The story of Curley, of Reynolds, what the wounded said . . . A hundred messengers working all bent on giving the story to the world, one newspaper writer and two telegraph operators. That story cost the *New York Herald* $3,000. It was worth the money. It was the greatest scoop ever known in newspaper circles. It was the finest job of reporting ever done on the American continent. Porter, the hero of Little Big Horn, was one of the most interesting features in it . . ."

Despite all this super human effort two Montana newspapers, the *Bozeman Times* and the *Helena Herald,* were the first to print the news of the Custer disaster. The *Bozeman Times* was first, having published an extra on July 3, 1876 followed by the *Helena Herald* on the fourth of July. The editor of the *Helena Herald* sent the news to the *Associated Press* in Salt Lake City and they in turn, relayed the news to the east where it made the late editions of several eastern papers on July 5, 1876. All of these publications scooped Colonel Clement Lounsberry's *Bismarck Tribune*; however, the *Tribune* was the first paper to publish an account that listed the dead and wounded of the battle.

Lieutenant Charles Lawrence Gurley of the 6th U.S. Infantry told in the same article from the *Record* that we have been following, how the news of Custer's defeat was received at Fort Abraham Lincoln shortly after the *Far West* tied up. Gurley says: "The news came to us about 2 A.M. Captain William S. McCaskey, Twentieth Infantry, summoned all the officers to his quarters at once, and there read to them the communication he had just received — per steamer *Far West*, from Captain Smith, General Terry's adjutant general. After we had recovered from the shock, Captain McCaskey requested us to assist him in breaking the news to the widows. It fell to my lot to accompany Captain McCaskey and Dr. J. V. D. Middleton, our post surgeon, to the quarters of Mrs. Custer — immediately east of those occupied by myself. We started on our sad errand a little before 7 o'clock on that 6th of July morning. I went to the rear of the Custer house, woke up Maria, Mrs. Custer's housemaid, and requested her to rap on Mrs. Custer's door, and say to her that she and Mrs. [Margaret] Calhoun[8] and Miss [Emma] Reed[9] were wanted in the parlor. On my way through the hall to open the front door, I heard the opening of the door of Mrs. Custer's room. She had been awakened by the footsteps in the hall. She called me by name and asked me the cause of my early visit. I made no reply, but followed Captain McCaskey and Dr. Middleton into the parlor. There we were almost immediately followed by the ladies of the Custer household, and there we told to them their first intimation of the awful result of the battle of the Little Big Horn.

"Imagine the grief of those stricken women, their sobs, their flood of tears. The grief that knew no consolation. The fearful depression that had hung over the fort for the past two days had its explanation then. It was almost stifling. Men and women moved anxiously, nervously, straining their eyes for the expected messenger, listening as footsteps fell. There was whispering and excitement among the Indian police. There were rumors of a great battle. Those who saw the Indians and witnessed their movements knew that something unusual must have happened. But what? Who would not give worlds to know just why all this excitement among the Indians? Fleet-footed warriors, mounted on still fleeter animals, aided perhaps by signals, had brought the news even before the *Far West* came, but no white man knew. That it brought joy to them was reason enough why it should have brought depression to the whites."

Epilogue

The Centennial in Philadelphia — 1876 News of the Custer Defeat Stuns Nation

1876 marked the Centennial of the Declaration of Independence. At an exhibition at Fairmount Park in Philadelphia the United States climaxed the celebration of their one hundredth anniversary.

The 1976 Bi-Centennial of the United States centered once again, as in 1876, on Philadelphia as the birthplace of the Declaration of Independence. In 1876 the Centennial Exhibition in Philadelphia was the highlight of all the celebrations. This exhibition lasted for six months, from May to November and was seen by twenty per cent of all Americans.

In one hundred years the United States had grown from a population of ten million inhabitants to over forty million. The Centennial was a time for reflection. A time to look back on the progress made in all areas of public and private enterprise. It was a time for showing off a dazzling array of spectacular examples of material abundance. It was a time, not unlike today, for wondering what we were going to do with all of those things.

In was July 6th when the news of the Custer defeat reached Philadelphia and the impact of this news upon all Americans was extraordinary.

Brevet General George A. Custer was known to everyone. His exploits during the Civil War were common knowledge,

106

his reputation as an Indian fighter was unparalleled. It was inconceivable that Custer and five companies of the elite Seventh Cavalry could be destroyed, wiped out by, what the sophisticated easterners termed, savages.

As more details of the battle became available and confirmation of the rumor of Custer's death became fact, Centennial visitors wondered aloud just how far we had progressed in the last one hundred years.

It was during this period of national trauma that monuments were proposed and built, songs and poems were written, stories and even a biography appeared that were dedicated to the man, Custer. Much of the original news was erroneous but it was this information on which the legend of Custer grew and flourished.

It has been two hundred years since the Declaration of Independence was written in 1776 and while we celebrate this magnificent document and reflect on the amazing accomplishments of this nation and examine our weaknesses we will be reminded that one hundred years have passed since Lt. Colonel George A. Custer and five companies of the Seventh Cavalry were defeated on the Little Big Horn River in Montana Territory.

As if George Custer himself had planned it, the Bi-Centennial of the United States and the Centennial of the Custer battle coincide and, as in 1876, the memory of the golden haired boy general has an undeniable influence on this national celebration.

Observances during the Custer Centennial focus on white man and red man alike and remind us how far we have come since the accounts of the courage and barbarism of both sides were first recorded and how far we have to go to achieve a true understanding and appreciation of diverse cultures.

Acknowledgements

In the summer of 1973, while in Billings, Montana on a promotional tour for my book, *Fort Custer on the Big Horn*, it was my good fortune to meet, again, Montana's foremost living Western artist, J. K. Ralston. It was then that this talented westerner suggested this project be undertaken. It has been a pleasure to work with Ken Ralston and I appreciated greatly and took advantage of his specialized knowledge on certain points.

Again, I am indebted to my resourceful wife, Frankie, for bringing the same constructive criticism to this endeavor that is her characteristic in the field of education.

It is especially pleasing to me to observe my two sons, Kip and Jim, as they embark on research projects of their own concerning significant events of the early west.

A special debt is owed the authors of the articles quoted within this volume. These adventurers tell what it was like during those exciting days. The stories are told without my interpretation. I leave it to others to tell what these writers "really meant."

Especially helpful were others who not only gave me their time but provided me with papers and documents that were of much help in the telling of this story. Among them were: The Custer Battlefield Museum and Historical Association, Crow Agency, Montana; John M. Carroll, New Brunswick, New Jersey; Robert Yellowtail, Lodge Grass, Montana; Frank Mercatante, Grand Rapids, Michigan; Charles A. Sweeney, President, Big Horn County State Bank, Hardin, Montana; J. D. Young, past Historian, Custer Battlefield National Monument; Harriett C. Meloy, Montana Historical Society; Myrtle Cooper, Reference Librarian, Parmly Billings (Mont.) Memorial Library; Mrs. Don C. Foote and John E. Foote of Billings, Montana.

Others who helped in many different ways and for whom I have the utmost respect are: Jim Willert, Glendora, California; Mike Reynolds, Hamilton, Montana; Kiah Buckner, Crow Agency, Montana; Hank Weibert, Garryowen, Montana; Kathryn Wright, Billings, Montana; John Popovich, Billings, Montana; George G. Osten, Billings, Montana; John Willard, Billings, Montana; and Hugh Schick of North Hollywood, California.

Of course, the above mentioned people share no responsibility for my thoughts and conclusions, no blame for my errors or inadequacies but only all the credit for whatever new understanding may emerge from the telling of *The Custer Adventure*.

Richard Upton
El Segundo, California

Bibliography

Documentary Sources

Parmly Billings Memorial Library, Billings, Montana
Custer Battlefield National Monument, Crow Agency, Montana
El Segundo Public Library, El Segundo, California
Montana Historical Society, Helena, Montana

Newspapers

Kansas
  Leavenworth Weekly Times, August 18, 1881
Minnesota
  St. Paul, *Pioneer - Press,* May 19, 1883
Montana
  Billings Gazette, June 25, 1923
New York
  New York Herald, July 30, 1876

Books and Articles

Amaral, Anthony A. *Comanche.* Los Angeles: Westernlore Press, 1961

Bradley, Lt. James H. *The March of the Montana Column.* Norman: University of Oklahoma Press, 1961

Brininstool, E. A. *Troopers With Custer.* Harrisburg, Pa.: The Stackpole Co., 1952

Brown, Dee. *The Year of the Century: 1876.* New York: Charles Scribner's Sons, 1966

Custer, Elizabeth B. *Boots and Saddles.* New York: Harper and Brothers, Franklin Square, 1885.

Gibbon, Colonel John. "Last Summer's Expedition Against The Sioux and Its Great Catastrophe," and "Hunting Sitting Bull," *The American Catholic Quarterly Review,* Vol. II, April and October 1877; reprint, Fort Collins, Colo.: The Old Army Press, 1969.

110

Godfrey, General Edward Settle. "Custer's Last Battle," *Century Magazine*, vol. 43, no. 3 (Jan. 1892), pp. 358-387.

Graham, Colonel W. A. *The Custer Myth.* Harrisburg, Pa.: The Stackpole Co., 1953.

Hammer, Kenneth. *Little Big Horn Biographies.* Custer Battlefield Historical and Museum Assn., 1964

Hanson, Joseph Mills, *The Conquest of the Missouri.* Chicago: A. C. McClurg and Co., 1909.

Heitman, Francis B. *Historical Register and Dictionary of the United States Army Vol. I.* Washington D.C.: University of Illinois Press, 1965.

Kuhlman, Dr. Charles. *Legend Into History.* Harrisburg, Pa.: The Stackpole Co., 1951.

Lounsberry, Clement. "Dr. H. R. Porter, Thrilling Incidents in the Life of a Bismarck Physician, A Remarkable Steamboat Ride," *Plains Talk, State Historical Society of North Dakota Newsletter,* Vol. 3, no. 4 (Fall 1972).

Luce, Edward S. "The Diary and Letters of Dr. James M. DeWolf," in *North Dakota History,* vol. 25, nos. 2 and 3 (April-July 1958) reprint of N.D.

McVey, Everett E. *The Crow Scout Who Killed Custer.* Billings, Montana: Privately printed, 1952.

Stewart, Edgar I. *Custer's Luck.* Norman: University of Oklahoma Press, 1955.

Terry, General Alfred H. *The Field Diary of General Alfred H. Terry, The Yellowstone Expedition - 1876.* Bellevue, Neb.: The Old Army Press, N.D.

Utley, Robert M. *Custer and the Great Controversy.* Los Angeles: Westernlore Press, 1962

Utley, Robert M. *The Reno Court of Inquiry.* Fort Collins, Colo.: The Old Army Press, 1972.

Footnotes

CHAPTER 1

1. Lt. Colonel George Custer's sister was married to Lt. James Calhoun, commanding officer of Company L. Calhoun died with his company at the Little Big Horn on June 25, 1876.

2. Women, mostly enlisted men's wives, who earned extra income by taking in laundry.

3. Heart River

CHAPTER 2

1. A rough fort-type construction located on the south bank of the Yellowstone River above the mouth of Glendive Creek built by troops under the command of Colonel David S. Stanley for the purpose of protecting survey parties of the Northern Pacific Railroad. Custer and ten companies of the 7th Cavalry were present on the 1873 expedition.

2. *Far West* and *Josephine*

3. This is an obvious mistake. Terry's diary states that it was June 19 that the dispatches were received.

4. Terry's field diary entry for June 19 says that, "Reno gave . . . no reason for his disobedience of orders." Custer was very angry with Reno for his failure to pursue the Indian trail and for not, at least, finding the number of Indians and the direction they were going. He also felt that Reno's troops might have alerted the Indians as to the soldiers' whereabouts.

5. The Gatling guns were a liability on the Reno scout and proved impractical with Gibbon and his column. The terrain of the area and a lack of healthy horses to pull the guns were formidable obstacles to overcome.

6. Terry meant the Big Horn River. The Little Big Horn empties into the Big Horn about 33 miles up the Big Horn River.

7. DeWolf is referring to the Reno scout on which he served. His 285 miles marched is a simple mathematical error in addition. According to his own mileage figures for the daily marches, the outfit traveled 241 miles.

112

8. Porter was also an Acting Assistant Surgeon assigned to the Seventh Cavalry.

9. From this incident the stories of drunkenness in Custer's command during the final battle evolved.

10. Gibbon's command was on the north bank of the Yellowstone opposite the mouth of the Rosebud.

11. Gatling guns.

12. Dr. Lord was killed with Custer on June 25, 1876.

13. Harrington's remains were never found after the Custer fight on June 25, 1876. He was presumed killed. He was in Company C., Seventh Cavalry.

14. Hodgson was killed when Reno's outfit re-crossed the Little Big Horn in its attempt to get to the high ground and then make a stand.

CHAPTER 3

1. Both of Company G, McIntosh was killed in the valley fight with Reno, June 25, 1876. Wallace was killed at the Battle of Wounded Knee, December 29, 1890.

2. This is incorrect. Bob Tail Bull, killed in the valley fight, was the leader of the Arikara scouts.

3. The spot, a favorite lookout point for the Crows when on horse-raiding parties later became known as the Crows' Nest. The Crow Indian scouts under the command of Lt. Chas. A. Varnum said they could see the Sioux village in the valley of the Little Big Horn.

4. Custer did not go to the Crows' Nest but to a spot nearby where the view of the valley was similar.

5. Most of the Indians say that the attack was a complete surprise. It is true that the column was seen by hunting parties of the Sioux but these Indians never reported the presence of the troops to the village. It is probable that the Indians thought that these troops were those of General Crook who they, the Indians, had already defeated on June 17, 1876 in the Battle of the Rosebud and therefore held no fear for them.

6. Sitting Bull had subjected himself to the rigors of the Sun Dance shortly before the Custer fight. During the supreme physical test he envisioned soldiers falling into his camp, upside down.

7. Yates commanded Company F and was killed June 25, 1876 at the Little Big Horn.

8. Shortly after leaving this water hole the first of two known messengers from Custer appeared. He was Sergeant Daniel Kanipe of Co. C with a message for the pack-train which at that moment was struggling in the morass. He was sent by Custer with an order to the pack-train to hurry it up. As he passed Benteen's column he called out, "We've got em boys." Not long after this Trumpeter John Martin arrived with his famous message from Lt. Colonel Custer to Capt. Benteen. This message read as follows: "Benteen, Come on. Big Village. Be quick. Bring packs." It was signed by Custer's adjutant Lt. W. W. Cooke and had a postscript: "bring pacs." This message is now in the library of the United States Military Academy at West Point.

9. It is possible that Keogh and Cooke were ordered by Custer to accompany Reno's column to the crossing and report back to Custer whether or not the crossing was successful.

CHAPTER 4

1. About this time Reno sent a second messenger to Custer. Trooper John Mitchell carried the same report that McIlhargey carried earlier, i.e. the enemy was in front and was strong. Both couriers were found killed with Custer.

2. The sixteen Arikara scouts were on the far left of the skirmish line set up by Reno's battalion. They made a valiant attempt to run off the Sioux pony herds but failed because they were badly outnumbered. The losses of the scouts were greater, in proportion, to the soldiers as five Indians were either killed or wounded.

3. The anticipated charge to the village proved to be a rumor. Shortly after this a charge or retreat to a defensive position atop the bluffs across the Little Big Horn was effected with disastrous results.

4. Many troopers, especially Company G, failed to hear any order to mount their horses and knew of no such maneuver until they saw others leaving the timber. Bloody Knife, an Arikara scout and a favorite of Custer's was killed by a volley of bullets fired by a large party of Sioux. Reno, who was about eight or ten feet to the left and rear of him was splattered by the blood and brains of the Arikara scout. George Herendeen, a civilian scout and courier, attributed this traumatic event as the cause of Reno's conflicting orders of dismount and mount and that the Indian's death was the principal factor in what turned into a stampede for the bluffs across the river.

114

5. "Lonesome Charley" Reynolds was one of those that was left behind in the timber. He tried to overtake the others but was killed in the valley while attempting to warn others of the danger. Reynolds was a superb guide in whom Custer had the utmost confidence. He never received the public recognition that some other guides did but was highly respected among his colleagues. Black interpreter Isaiah Dorman's death during this race towards the river was described by Sioux Chief Runs-the-Enemy like this: "We passed a black man in a soldier's uniform and we had him. He turned on his horse and shot an Indian right through the heart. Then the Indians fired at this one man and riddled his horse with bullets. His horse fell over on his back and the black man could not get up. I saw him as I rode by. I afterwards saw him lying there dead." Lt. Benjamin "Benny" Hodgson, Reno's adjutant and a popular member of the regiment was left in the timber also. Recovering quickly he mounted his horse and raced to the river crossing where, in mid-stream, he was hit in the leg by a Sioux bullet that also killed his horse. A trooper seeing his plight, held out a stirrup to Hodgson and towed him to the opposite bank. Hodgson was killed by an Indian marksman as he was ascending the ravine that led to Reno's new defensive position.

6. In substance, various accounts report Varnum as saying, "For God's sake, boys, don't run. Don't let them whip us. We must go back and save the wounded." To which Major Reno, who Varnum did not see, replied testily, "I am in command here, Sir." Varnum then said nothing more and joined Company A.

CHAPTER 5

1. Reno, at the 1879 Court of Inquiry, put the total at 114 but he didn't include the officers or Indian scouts. There were probably about 140 men in all.

2. This was Custer and his five companies of the Seventh Cavalry.

3. DeRudio, as Captain Frederick Benteen would say, "embellished" his story at this point. O'Neill put the total at 50 shots fired.

4. This was the fight on Reno Hill in progress.

CHAPTER 6

1. The Indians, seeing that Reno no longer posed a threat to the village, had left to meet the new challenge of Custer and his command that had appeared downstream opposite the Indian village.

2. About this time firing, in the form of distinct volleys, was heard coming from downstream in the direction that Custer was last seen. At the Reno Court of Inquiry in 1879 many men, including Lt. Varnum, Dr. Porter, Captain Moylan, Lt. Edgerly, Lt. Godfrey and George Herendeen testified that they heard this firing. Benteen and Reno stated that they heard no such firing. Captain Thomas Weir, commanding Company D, hearing the gunfire, had become exasperated with Reno's reluctance to march to the sound of the guns and, without authority, took his company in the direction from which the firing appeared to be coming. Reaching a high point, now known as Weir Point, Indians could be seen riding around and firing at objects on the ground. Finally Reno organized the column and proceeded in the direction that Weir had taken.

3. Weir Point

4. Most accounts by survivors of the Reno Hill fight have said that at the time this incident was taking place no thought was given to the possibility of a disaster of the magnitude eventually discovered.

5. Ryan is mistaken here as burial parties later found no bodies near Medicine Tail Ford.

6. The retreat from Weir Point back to the original defensive position selected by Reno might have turned into another such debacle as happened in the valley if it wasn't for the quick thinking of Lt. Godfrey who deployed his company as skirmishers and slowed the Indian attack allowing the column to set up defensively before the full force of the Indian attack was felt.

7. Eighteen men volunteered to go to the river to obtain water, especially for the wounded men who were suffering terribly. Using canteens and camp kettles to obtain water for their comrades on the hill the troopers braved a withering fire from the Indians at almost point-blank range. For this courageous act all eighteen troopers received the Medal of Honor.

8. A young warrior, coupstick in hand, dashed towards the soldiers' line and attempted to count coups on the trooper's body. For his effort the Indian was shot dead.

9. Later, the Indian stories all deny having taken any prisoners. During Reno's attack on the village at least two troopers lost control of their horses and were carried unwillingly through the Indian lines into the village. Perhaps these could be the remains of these unlucky men.

116

CHAPTER 7

1. This was the Battle of the Rosebud that took place on June 17, 1876 between General Crook and the Sioux and Cheyenne warriors. Crook, in addition to his own force, had 176 Crow Scouts fighting for him.

2. This is the "lone tepee" or "burning tepee" that is referred to many times in reports and accounts of the Custer battle. When Custer and his forces discovered this tepee some mistook the elaborate decorations and Indian signs as a warning to the soldiers when, in fact, it was the Indian custom to decorate the burial lodge of a fallen warrior.

3. The troopers had been paid at the first camp after leaving Fort Abraham Lincoln on May 17, 1876.

CHAPTER 8

1. J. K. Ralston, noted Montana artist and illustrator of this book, knew descendents of the half-blood Sioux Indian interpreter and informs us that the spelling of the name should be "Mitch Bruyer."

2. There were two more Crow Scouts, Half Yellow Face and White Swan, but through some misunderstanding, they left Custer and joined Reno shortly after Reno crossed the Little Big Horn River and began his charge towards the village.

CHAPTER 9

1. The remains of these two officers along with Lt. Henry M. Harrington were never identified.

2. At least one animal was found alive on Custer ridge. Comanche, Capt. Myles Keogh's horse, was discovered badly wounded. For sentimental reasons Comanche was transported, with the wounded soldiers, on the steamer *Far West* back to Fort Abraham Lincoln where the animal was nursed back to health and lived out its life as a very special member of the Seventh Cavalry.

3. This officer was Lt. James Bradley.

4. Lt. Luther R. Hare and Lt. George D. Wallace.

5. Weir Point

6. Capt. Frederick W. Benteen's Company H

7. Capt. Frederick W. Benteen

8. The exact total was three.

9. Exact numbers are impossible to calculate as the company rosters were kept by the first sergeants and were lost when the Indians stripped and looted the fallen soldiers. About 14 soldiers were never accounted for, but occasionally while maintenance work is performed at the present Custer Battlefield National Monument, the remains of a soldier are found.

10. About 220.

11. About midway between Custer Hill and Weir Point and about 600 yards east of the Medicine Tail crossing the isolated body of Company L First Sergeant James Butler was found. Speculation has been made as to whether or not Butler was used as a messenger during the last desperate stages of the battle.

12. Henry Bostwick and Pvt. James E. Goodwin

13. A year later in 1877, Lt. Doane selected this plateau for the site of Fort Custer.

14. Hanson, *The Conquest of the Missouri,* p. 291.

CHAPTER 10

1. Comanche, Capt. Myles Keogh's horse and the only living survivor of the Custer fight found on the battlefield was placed on the deck of the *Far West* where, under special care, it began its road to recovery from wounds suffered during the fight.

2. The engineer was George Foulk.

3. Private William George of Company H was buried near the mouth of Powder River.

4. Goose, an Arikara scout who had his right hand severely injured, was put off at Fort Buford.

5. At Fort Stevenson, on General Terry's orders, the *Far West's* derrick and jack-staff was draped in black and the flag flown at half-mast.

6. The distance covered was actually 710 miles.

118

7. Kellogg, a newspaper correspondent from the *Bismarck Tribune,* was killed with Custer. Near Kellogg's body were found his notebooks.

8. Custer's sister and wife of Lt. James Calhoun, Co. L, who was killed with Custer.

9. A niece of Lt. Colonel George A. Custer whose brother Henry Armstrong (Autie) Reed was killed at the Little Big Horn. Boston Custer, another brother of Lt. Colonel George A. Custer, accompanied the expedition and was killed at the Little Big Horn.